Hoosier Farmers
in a
New Day

BY EDNA MOORE COLBY

Published by
Indiana Farm Bureau, Inc., Indianapolis

iv

Publisher's Foreword and Dedication

"Hoosier Farmers In A New Day" is published in 1968 at the direction of the Board of Directors and officers of Indiana Farm Bureau, Inc. as part of the commemoration of the Fiftieth Anniversary of the founding of the organization in March, 1919.

This record of the formation, growth and development of a farm organization which has become a potent force in public affairs is dedicated to the real heroes in the battle for Equality For Agriculture—the thousands of present and past Farm Bureau members and leaders throughout Indiana.

These pioneers have made the past fifty years Golden Years of accomplishment in Hoosier agriculture. They are the heroes—sung and unsung—who have been and still are the chief beneficiaries of their own united efforts.

GEORGE DOUP, *President*
Indiana Farm Bureau, Inc.

A Word From The Governor

I congratulate the Indiana Farm Bureau upon its 50th anniversary, and I commend the Bureau for recording its remarkable story in this book.

This is more than a story of the Farm Bureau. It is the story also of the Hoosier farmer in times of economic distress, in his struggle for equality, in the amazing technological advances increasing productivity and quality, and his new role as a practitioner of agri-business.

Mrs. Edna Moore Colby has written this story well. She wields her pen cleverly and concisely, giving hard facts and at the same time entertaining the reader by amusing anecdotes. She has captured the character of the Hoosier farmer as he faced his days in the last 50 years.

The Indiana Farm Bureau should be proud indeed of its record of achievement. Its force in improving the agricultural economy has been reflected in a better life for all Hoosiers. Its public actions always have been constructive and responsible. I wish the Indiana Farm Bureau another illustrious 50 years.

ROGER D. BRANIGIN
Governor of Indiana

May 24, 1968

Acknowledgements

In attempting a book of this kind, I was from the outset faced with many problems. First, there is a surplus of information. The question became what shall be included and what left out.

The story of an organization is, first of all, the story of people, their aspirations and their desperations, and most certainly the goals which brought them together and held them together. This story of people must underwrite the cold statistics of Indiana Farm Bureau's development.

The book should project the broad scope envisioned by the organization's founders. It must convince beyond doubt that the original concept and the present program are equal to all farm problems; and that solutions arrived at by all will not hurt some. The book must demonstrate that all farmers joined together can achieve what smaller groups dare not attempt.

I decided that the book must also interpret the character of the organization and examine its role in agriculture. Where is it succeeding.

Many details have been omitted of necessity. There is sure to be disagreement on some of the story that is here related; but I believe, that in matters of importance, it is accurate.

I looked to the memories of charter members in many parts of the state for the information I needed. I have studied the pages of The HOOSIER FARMER, which published its first copy in June, 1919, the year the Indiana Farm Bureau was born. I have turned to official minutes of annual conventions to catch the flavor of the arguments that abounded on many issues. Minutes of meetings of the boards of directors, held at critical junctures in the organization's growth, have been studied.

In all this research, the exercise of personal judgment, guided by the advice of present state leaders, has had to be the final determinant. I feel the picture presented herein is a true one. To me it is an inspiring and a rousing one.

While there have been many and vigorous differences of opinion along the way, that vigor itself is an evidence of good leadership. The process of problem solving remains the same today as when Farm Bureau started. The only difference is that the wheels of the machinery have been oiled in today's process.

I am greatly indebted to many persons who have given generously of their time to help keep the record straight. Among these persons are: Hassil E. Schenck, the late Mrs. Charles W. Sewell, the late J. Walter Thompson, Anson S. Thomas, Marvin J. Briggs, Mr. and Mrs. Chauncey Downey, I. H. Hull, Larry Brandon, Harry Truax, the late Claude Wickard, L. E. Hoffman, the late Albert Ferris, Guy Cantwell, George W. Elliott, the late Oscar Swank, and the late Edmond (Jack) Foust, one time editor of The HOOSIER FARMER, who compiled a body of information on the Farm Bureau years up until his death in 1945.

I am also indebted to C. W. Stall, current director of information and public relations, Indiana Farm Bureau, Inc., for his consultations and assistance but particularly for his diligence and efforts to update my manuscript on what took place after I finished the original draft in 1964. His work in handling innumerable details pertaining to the publication of the book is greatly appreciated.

It is my sincere hope that older members of Farm Bureau will urge the younger ones to read the book, so they may fully appreciate the fact that the organization did not come into existence full blown like the mythological Minerva from the head of Jupiter; but that it came through great travail to its present status as an agricultural institution of great influence and accomplishment.   E.M.C.

Contents

Chapter IV—Years of Travail

Chapter V—Other Ventures

Chapter VI—Influence in State Legislature

Chapter VII—Firmly Established

Addenda

+++

Chapter I

The Stage Is Set

+++

The National Scene

Woodrow Wilson as president of the United States had just led this nation through the First World War, a victory which, it had been promised, would "make the world safe for democracy."

Business titans such as J. P. Morgan, who flung his millions about, and Henry Ford, who reinvested his profits in an expanding industry and was the first to give his workers five dollars per day,—these were the types riding the economic arc on Morgan's slogan: Don't sell America short.

Samuel Gompers had succeeded in forming a labor organization potentially able to hold its own against the industrial giants of the times. Galli-Curci's rich soprano warmed capacity audiences in Chicago and New York Opera Houses. Babe Ruth hit 50 home runs in 1920 to salvage baseball from near death at the hands of the Chicago Black Sox scandal.

The facade which the nation presented to the world was exciting and prosperous. The economy was jumping up and down like a young boy on a pogo stick. Businessmen took advantage of both bull and bear markets.

But for the man on the land trying to make a living for his family after World War I, prices moved in one direction only, downward, leaving him with an appalling fear of the future.

Farmers were the first victims of the war's aftermath. In Indiana their new and struggling organization was to be put to the test. That organization, now called The Indiana Farm Bureau, had barely gotten started toward the realization of a very ambitious program under these very trying circumstances. The fact that it survived is testimony to the caliber of its founders. They came out fighting.

Two farm neighbors who liked to recall those early days had come out to bask in the morning sunshine. Come to that time of life which gives respite from activity, they found themselves, strangely enough, nearly always in agreement. It had not once been so. Now their past differences were something to muse upon and laugh about.

The early May sun came in on a direct line to the Indiana countryside. There was not a cloud to deflect it. It lavished its warmth, after a biting winter, much like a wise parent who scolds, then caresses his child. As they basked in this spring bonus, John said:

"No, sir; if anyone had told me 50 years ago what today's farmer would be like, I wouldn't 've believed him. But, look at 'im. He's really joined the human race, you might say . . . But we had some real tooth and nail battles in those days."

He settled back in his porch chair and chewed on his pipe a bit. He was talking to a man who had been around almost as long as he had. Though their faces were furrowed like the land across the highway, their eyes twinkled with certain triumph. Those early days "were really tough."

"The national convention I attended last winter was an eye opener," recalled Mort, the younger one. "I hadn't been to one for a long time . . . One of the Indiana delegates stood up and made a speech at a time when it was needed. Everybody listened. There, in that big auditorium before thousands from all over the country, it was like one farmer saying things we all believed in. You could have heard a pin drop. It got to me, clear down to my shoe laces."

There are still, in this state, hundreds of Farm Bureau charter members living, who remember the hardships and the joys of those days,—the physical hardships and the joys of accomplishment.

Life On The Farm

In the springtime of the present century, farm families found their social outlets in an occasional barn raising and the big community dinner that followed; or at the threshing ring supper with all the ice cream you could eat; or at the box supper at the district school, when girls and young women, with artfully decorated and amply filled boxes, vied for a young swain's bashful bidding. Very few older people in rural Indiana have not heard the "Now I have three, who'll give me four?" chant of the box supper auctioneer.

Women often gathered in the early part of this century for a carpet rag cutting or a quilting bee. This occurred in homes and the hostess, who was to benefit from the help of her neighbors' needles and scissors, would serve cake and coffee; or, if it were an all-day meeting as happened frequently, there would be a complete dinner at noon. The modern nutritionist would have characterized such meals as protein and calorie-packed.

When rural free delivery of mail was enacted by Act of Congress in 1896, it did not immediately reach all areas. The necessary personnel to implement it had to be found. In many farm homes, it

was custom for the head of the house to go to town on Saturday to get the mail that had accumulated through the week. One Farm Bureau charter member recalls how he always looked forward to receiving The Youth's Companion. "There's nothing like it today," he said nostalgically.

As is man's wont, hungry minds were reaching out for learning beyond their narrow confines. The introduction of the county agricultural agent and his new knowledge of farming, which at first seemed like magic to some but only dubious 'book larnin' to others, broke the back of inefficient farming. Men, who had planted by the moon or as their fathers had done, now began to see new methods demonstrated and seed stocks improved in a vast and glowing promise of better things to come.

Culture clubs dotted the state and often included farm people. In them, the members often studied agriculture besides literature and current public problems. One such problem was the effect of the immigrant on the American way of life. Suspicion and distrust were building up against the immigrant who a few years before had seen his kinsmen supply the labor which got the wheels of the new industrial revolution rolling. It was not just numbers which rural and city people alike feared, as subsequent restrictive legislation proved. The Immigration Act of 1924 limited by quota the number of people to be admitted from each country with Great Britain being given much the largest quota.

Newspaper accounts of these local group discussions bear witness to the fact that rural people once abetted this sentiment. Yet today the Mexican immigrant is invited, yes urged, to come into the state to help tend and harvest farm crops. So swings that unpredictable force called public sentiment.

These local culture groups even weighed the new socialism, we are told, and conducted debates on its values.

The old shell of isolationism that had so long stigmatized the farmer was being punctured by inquiry and interest on every hand.

On the heels of this interest were formed Farmers' Institutes, one of the first efforts in adult education. Set up by Purdue University before the Extension Service was established, the Institutes brought to the rural community a diverse array of topics for study by farm leaders. Purdue provided some of the instructors from its staff and employed others from among lay farmers reputed to be well informed.

Each lecturer had a repertoire of subjects from which local people chose what they wanted to hear. The community had to insure the number of "students" required before it could get the Institute to come to its midst. Each enrollee paid a nominal fee for the short course. The Institute was usually held in a schoolhouse or some other community center.

Although this early attempt at adult education benefited relatively few persons in a neighborhood, it did make a definite contribution to the whole of agriculture. It was at the Institute that farm leaders promoted clubs for farm children, primarily for the practice and demonstration of better farming methods. These clubs, later known as 4-H, spread like wildfire to cast the child as teacher of the man,— often a reluctant pupil.

Others at the Institutes began to argue for a farm organization that would truly represent their economic and legislative interests. One such 'visionary' was Lewis Taylor of Warrick county, an Institute lecturer, who nearly twenty years later was to become president of the Indiana Farm Bureau, Inc.

Other farm leaders who served as instructors at the Institutes were: Mrs. Taylor, Albert Ferris, Wayne county; Mrs. Charles W. Sewell, Benton county; Addison Drake, Sullivan county; Guy Cantwell, Owen county; Maurice Douglas and Mr. and Mrs. Calvin Perdue, Shelby county; W. F. Franklin, Hendricks county; C. R. Benjamin, Lake county; Mrs. C. N. Lindley, Washington county; Oscar Swank, Tippecanoe county; H. M. Widney, St. Joseph county; and M. J. Briggs, then of Miami county. There were perhaps others whose names could not be ascertained.

The Institute program did not always run smoothly. The story is told that in one county it had been decided (apparently without the pastor's knowledge) to hold the event in the church.

The small band of farm people, bent on learning, trudged along the creek bed as the shortest route to the church, only to find the doorway blocked by the minister.

"Anything that occurs in this church that is not sanctioned by me is the work of the devil," he glowered.

In another county, an Institute gathering found it advisable to recess for the funeral of one of the locally esteemed citizens. They withdrew to the cemetery to find the grave had not yet been dug. Each man took his turn with hastily recruited spades while they waited for the mourners to arrive.

The Institutes, Better Farming Associations, and other study groups stirred the soil for the vigorous general farm organization that was to follow. Many changes were taking place. The farmer's imagination had been caught, and these initial efforts in adult education were largely responsible.

Organization Needed

Developments off the farm before 1919 had set an example of effective cooperation. Labor was becoming tightly knit into trade unions whose influence was being watched with a degree of trepidation. Big business had learned that by becoming bigger still it could conceivably control its source of supply for needed raw materials, and so could expect to exercise authority over costs.

The war had also proved that people could work together effectively if they had common cause.

Non-farm leaders were also urging farmers to

organize "across the board" for educational, legislative and social reasons, and to do anything else
that was honorable to improve the business of
agriculture. The idea took hold like a prairie fire.
Indiana was the first to join the American Farm
Bureau Federation, although several states were
ahead of her in organizing.

Another factor which fed the early growth of
these farm groups was possibly their need for social
recognition. The old concept in Europe, from which
many of their ancestors had emigrated,—the concept
that a farmer was no more than a peasant—was
fiercely resented by American farmers who occasionally heard themselves referred to as "just
farmers."

They were not only farmers, they were distin-
guished individuals and proud citizens, the likes of
whom had settled these lands. They had dared when
others had quaked. They had cleared the forests and
seeded the fields, while lesser men sought sheltered
occupations. They were America itself!

This smouldering but fierce resentment forged
itself into an equally fierce loyalty to the cause of
agriculture. "Equality for agriculture" became the
demand of the newly organized Indiana Federation
of Farmers' Associations, later to be known as The
Indiana Farm Bureau, Inc.

This new band of stout-hearted men initially
spelled out its character and purpose in these words:

"An organization of the farmers, by the farmers, to protect the interests of farmers; and by education, legislation and other honorable means, to promote the largest good for all the people."

Aiding in the early and very trying days of the organization were the county agricultural agents, who saw in it a tool which they could use in getting extension information to farmers. For more than a decade they had tried to contact the farmer individually on his land, an insurmountable task when one considers that there was only one agent for every two or three thousand farmers, and then only in those counties which had hired agents.

Several agents had been calling together informal groups for instruction. They called them Better Farming Associations. Some referred to them as bureaus, a word that had come into use from government parlance during World War I. Businessmen and bankers also referred to the associations as bureaus. Drawn together for a variety of reasons, they formed the nucleus of the Indiana Farm Bureau. There had been similar activity on the national scene. This was not an isolated rebellion, but a spontaneous, widespread demand through organization for equality for agriculture.

Reports from other states told of farmers organizing. Everywhere they had seen the merits of banding together in community drives for the war effort. Farmers had been active in these drives.

They were convinced of the value of cooperative action.

As early as 1916, a Farmers' National Congress was held in Indianapolis. Those attending were told to return to their states and organize farmers. When Will Averitt, Johnson county, who attended the Congress told his county agent what was proposed, he was asked: "Why not organize Johnson county first?" Mr. Averitt claims that honor for his county.

Liberty Hyde Bailey of Cornell University was on early instigator of farmer organization. In fact, the first national meeting that had a direct bearing on the incubating Farm Bureau was held at Ithaca, New York, where Cornell is situated.

While the National Grange had been in existence many years prior to this time, Indiana farmers regarded it as a wholly respectable but fraternal organization. What they needed now, and desperately, was a voice to represent them before the lawmaking bodies of their state and nation, and one strong enough to promote their economic interests.

At Ithaca, this idea crystallized nationally. It was hoped that the proposed organization would include all farmers and serve all farmers. This across the board organization concept has inspired Indiana Farm Bureau leaders all through the years. Not until all farmers in the state become members, to be served by the organization and in turn to direct its program through policies reached by democratic action, will Farm Bureau leaders relax.

There were many, many problems confronting farmers in 1919 when the Indiana organization came into existence. A review of some of them may help the reader to understand the Farm Bureau program that has since developed.

Economic Conditions

Let's look briefly at economic conditions before the turn of this century and during the first twenty years. The movement of people from the east westward into new land continued from the beginning of the nineteenth century until 1900. For a time, from 1910 till 1914, the economy struck a happy balance.

Then like a great changing tide, people started going to the cities for higher wages brought on by the industrial revolution, exported here from England. The cities consequently were becoming vast social complexes where rising living costs were a matter of course. The price of manufactured items rose in response to demand created by higher wages and the greater investment required in new manufacturing equipment.

Whether a man can, to some degree, control his environment determines his success or failure. The city laboring man was learning how to use his union to negotiate or coerce his case for higher wages and shorter hours. A man employed in management, saw the cost of production determine selling price, profit and his salary.

On the other hand, the farmer could not, usually, name the price of what he sold; yet he must pay the going rate for what he bought to operate his farm. He has, with the help of the research scientist, acquired the ability to control many livestock and plant diseases and insects; and has learned to make use of more efficient methods of production. But he cannot control or predict with any accuracy — long in advance — the very critical factor of weather. He is only one of many small "manufacturers" of food, and is in an uncertain position when it comes to predicting what his products will bring at the marketplace.

Some farmers accept this element of risk and uncertainty as challenge; others fear its potential devastation. Too, the farm economy being basic is the first to feel economic fluctuations.

With the First World War came a drain of youth off the farm for military service. Many young men never returned, or if they did they came home with new ideas of what the big, wide world held in store for them. Discontent with farm life followed. The popular song, "How you Goin' To Keep 'Em Down On The Farm?" that hit the music halls at the time was a true reflection of the problem that had developed.

This migration of farm boys to the city to work left the farmers short of labor. They had to buy expensive machinery to replace the labor once supplied by their now departing sons.

By 1926, the rural population had a troublesome imbalance. There was a disproportionately large number of children under fifteen to educate and an insufficiency of those in the productive age bracket of fifteen to forty-five. In a population of thirty millions, according to census figures, cities had two million fewer children under ten than did rural areas. This fact alone was responsible for two related problems.

Farmers and small town residents had more children to educate in proportion to the number of taxpayers. Heavy school costs came to be borne in large part by property taxes. Thereby started a struggle for relief from high property taxes, a battle that continues till this day.

The farmer also found himself faced with higher operating costs, higher prices for clothing for his family, higher salaries for school teachers, higher fees for the doctor and the dentist. Yet he was producing more food per man hour of labor than ever before, without receiving a parity price for his products, or a price considered fair when measured by its purchasing power in the general economy.

Farm efficiency has been improving since the founding of the U.S. Department of Agriculture by Congress in the administration of Abraham Lincoln. At the new Land Grant Colleges and Experiment Stations which were then established, there began a scientific study of plant diseases, followed by such services as meat inspection, extension service program, and market reports to inform producers of economic trends. Subsequent market regulations, expanded credit, nutrition studies, conservation measures, and rural electrification, to name only a few of the highlights, aided in farm efficiency.

But this was still not enough to meet the economic nightmare of the twenties and thirties. Farmers, who had been encouraged to and lauded for producing an abundance of food during World War I, suddenly found themselves being reviled and blamed for the high cost of food. During the period, farmers had bought more high priced land to meet that demand. In fact, they had plowed up forty million acres of new land during the war. This laid the ground-work for producing the surpluses which were to harass the farmer in the decades since.

John G. Brown of Monon, the new Indiana farm organization's first president, went to Washington, D. C., in July, 1919, with five other state Farm Bureau presidents to confer with President Wilson in defense of the farmer against the charge being made that he was profiteering on food. This concern was evident in an early request of IFB leaders (in fact, at the April, 1919 organization meeting) that the U.S. Congress pass legislation to stabilize food prices.

Strangely enough, farmers were not benefiting from the high prices. It is a matter of record that at

Indiana Farm Bureau Presidents

(Above left):
John G. Brown
1919-1922

(Above right):
Wm. H. Settle
1923-1934

(Below left):
Lewis Taylor
1935-1936

(Below right):
Hassil E. Schenck
1937-1957

(Center):
George Doup
1958-

Indiana Farm Bureau's Board of Directors is composed of 13 members. Left to right, they are:

Virgil Cline, Selma, district 6; George Ruschhaupt, New Palestine, district 8; Linville Bryant, Versailles, district 10; Warren Wheaton, Oakland City, district 9; Edward Kuhn, Bicknell, district 7; Marion Cowan, Crawfordsville, district 5; Lawrence Holloway, Colfax, district 3; Oris Bedenkop, Westville, district 1; Glenn W. Sample, Zionsville, vice-president; President George Doup, Columbus; Mrs. Guy E. Gross, Churubusco, second vice-president; George Neff, Goshen, district 2; and Carlin Schoeff, Montpelier, district 4.

First FB Board of Directors were (left to right) standing: W. F. Franklin, Danville; F. P. Mullens, Alexandria; V. D. Sexton, Switz City; John J. Brown, Rockport; John G. Klein, North Vernon. (Seated): J. A. Warren, Kouts; Hugh M. Widney, St. Joe; C. W. Hickman, Lafayette; and H. T. Walker, Montpelier. Not shown is L. M. Vogler, Hope.

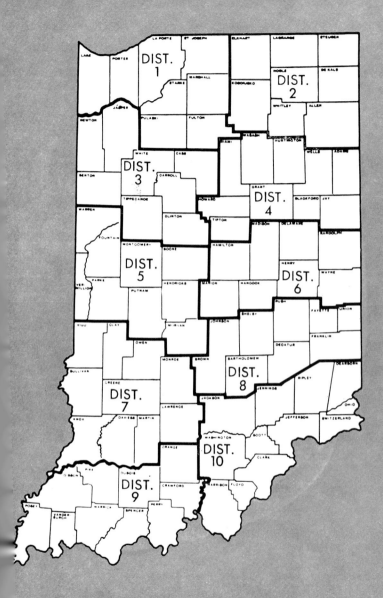

Ten Farm Bureau districts, ranging in size from 8 to 12 counties, provide the legal basis for electing state FB directors and woman leaders. These same geographical areas are observed by Farm Bureau Insurance companies, Indiana Farm Bureau Cooperative Association, and Producers Marketing Association (plus two districts in Illinois), thereby serving to bind FB and these affiliated services together in strength.

(Below): Heart beat of Indiana Farm Bureau is the annual delegate session where policy is made. Until World War II (1942) state conventions were held at Tomlinson Hall on East Market St. in Indianapolis, and since have required the larger facilities of the Murat Theatre (above) in the Capitol City.

the very time livestock prices were dropping, retail meat prices were rising. Nevertheless, these loose charges struck home.

War's disruptive forces were at work on the economy, too. Heretofore, we had been a debtor nation. The war converted us within a few short and tragic years into a creditor nation. Public pressure moved national leaders to ask our former military allies to start paying their war debts. Our national treasury was in need of money and this was the quickest way to get it.

Our demand for payment lost us most of our best foreign customers. Already hit by the devastation of war they, too, were short of money. Dollars applied to war debts could not buy our agricultural surplus (among other U.S. products); and so farm prices, with loss of exports, took a nose dive.

The urban community was not hit by these forces until several years after agriculture began to show signs of distress. The reason was simple. When industry turned to making consumer goods, after several years of manufacturing war material, it found a ready-made market. Domestic demand was ready and waiting.

On April 6, 1921, Henry A. Wallace, later to become Secretary of Agriculture and Vice-President of the U.S., predicted at an Iowa meeting of the swine industry: "The farm depression will be communicated to industry and business generally."

He proved painfully right. When agriculture's

contribution to the gross national product (total
income) declined, and the farmer's purchase of
city-made supplies stopped dead, then the entire
economy became strangled in the Great Depression.
National farm income dropped from $9 billion in
1920 to $2.5 billion in 1932.

The farm parity ratio in 1920 stood at 105. A
year later it had plummeted to 82. By 1932, corn
sold for 12 cents per bushel; hogs for 2½ cents a
pound, and wheat for 32 cents per bushel. Nearly
six per cent of the farms in the nation changed owners involuntarily during the Depression. In 1939
there were 740,000 farm families on relief in the U.S.

However, in the midst of despair farmers did not
quit producing. It can truthfully be said they fed the

nation out of their own pocketbooks, when prices were below the cost of production.

In 1932, a farmer had to sell fifty dozen eggs to pay his Farm Bureau membership dues.

Some farmers burned corn to heat their homes, because it was worth less than either coal or wood and did not have to be hauled from the nearest town. Wheat was used one year as admission to the Indiana State Fair, because farmers did not have cash. One bushel admitted an adult; a half bushel, a child

A northwestern Indiana farmer claims the truth of the story that he shipped some sheep to Chicago and received word from the commission agent that the animals did not bring enough to pay the shipping costs; so the farmer had to send cash to make up the difference.

In the depth of the Depression, Guy Cantwell, Owen county's first Farm Bureau president, reports that Harrison county, Indiana, teachers went without pay for three years.

This then is a glimpse at the background upon which the doggedly determined Indiana Farm Bureau laid its foundations.

Local Stirrings

Soon after the war, farmers noted the storm clouds with a sense of gloom. Something must be done. It remained up to them.

"On a Sunday morning, August 25, 1918," Thomas Downey tells us, "a handful of Warren county farmers met in Oscar Larm's front yard to see what could be done about the military services taking all the farm boys, at a time when we were being asked to produce enough food and fiber to supply the nation and its allies in the War." At that time, this was their most pressing problem.

Larm was asked to call upon the recruiting officer for the area. When he returned from this mission, he reported he had been told that labor and industry were organized, but no one was representing the farmers. This incident served to congeal the interest and determination of those Warren county farmers, who immediately banded together to become what was later the Warren County Farm Bureau, one of the first Indiana counties to organize. Their first president was Frank J. Goodwin.

According to Herbert A. Fields, Morgan county charter member, that county also organized the year before the state federation was formed. Morgan county commissioners were reluctant to appropriate enough money for the county agent's salary. One of that county Farm Bureau's first cooperative efforts was the donation of $700 for that purpose—to complement the agent's salary from the Federal government.

One of the greatest sources of irritation before Farm Bureau was formed was the shabby treatment given livestock at the Indianapolis stockyards. Many farmers shipped their animals to Indianapolis rather than sell them to a local buyer. They shipped in wagons, trucks, or rail cars, often to find at the terminal market there was no provision for their disposal. Hogs were allowed to die in transport vehicles, or were unloaded and allowed to die from exposure and neglect in the stockyards. It was charged that local packers were even buying in Louisville, Kentucky.

Grievances were aired at a meeting of a hundred farmers in Hendricks county in December, 1918. One man present told of seeing as many as fifty dead hogs removed from one rail car at the stockyards.

This gathering resulted in the organization of the Hendricks County Federation of Farmers, with W. F. Franklin as its first president. The group later became an early member of the Indiana Federation of Farmers' Associations.

There were many suggestions made at that December meeting in a desperate effort to correct stockyards' conditions. At this time, another cause of resentment was the contention of Samuel Gompers, national labor leader, that food prices were too high and laborers' wages too low, the inference being that farmers were profiteering. From every side, the farmer found himself on the defensive.

Some of these Hendricks county men suggested that farmers reduce their production of hogs. One even said that the government should set the price on pork for longer periods than a month at a time, so farmers could anticipate the market. But then, as now, most of them did not cotton to measures that would put a ceiling on their efforts. They began to see clearly that they would have to help themselves.

These meetings in the formative months of the organization were bleak affairs. A feeling of utter futility is best reflected by Larry Brandon, DeKalb county farmer, later district director, state organization director and vice-president, in telling of his first meeting. "Farm prices were falling. Mortgage foreclosures were on the increase. The first meeting I attended was in 1919. There were eight men present. With kerosene lanterns in hand, we sat around a box stove. We had left the women at home or with a neighbor. When I picked up Mrs. Brandon on the way home, she asked what we had done.

"We spit in the fire until it went out," I told her; "then we picked up our lanterns, locked the door, and started home!" One can feel the frustration and desperation that pervaded such events. The wonder is that those pioneers in the movement carried on beyond that point.

In many counties, farm groups were forming. More than likely they had not caught the big picture of what would or could come of their efforts. But they were hopeful.

"Everything was in the future, promises," says Anson Thomas, who was a Montgomery county farmer, livestock department employee, secretary of the state organization for a very brief period, and for thirty-one years a very effective legislative director of IFB.

Albert Ferris, twice Wayne County Farm Bureau president, who was at the time of the founding of the organization the master of his local Grange, says that it was the consensus of farmers that, though the Grange provided a social activity, it did not meet the expanding needs in "the larger field of purchasing, marketing, and legislation."

Scott Doup, older brother of incumbent IFB president George Doup and until 1964 manager of the Seymour Producers' Marketing Association for fifteen years, reports the same sentiment existed in Bartholomew county where he then resided. "The Indiana Grange did not seem aggressive enough to many in helping the farmer in solving his economic plight and in getting needed legislation."

Jacob Altepeter of Benton county says: "I think Farm Bureau was started in this county with the thought that we could go to the elevator and name the price for our grain and get it; but we found out it wouldn't work that way."

A number of counties found the county Commissioners unsympathetic with the farmer's request for a county agricultural agent. Through their new organization, he presented his case to the Commissioners and with the help of other farmer members, they talked (sometimes using political influence) with the county board of education, who had to approve of whatever agent would be employed. (The method of approval has since that time been modified.)

A number of county Farm Bureaus made it of primary concern to give money to this cause, because they were beginning to see tangible results from the Extension Service.

There were many inequities in the property tax system of some counties. An early county president reports that his organization (through his efforts) found two hundred properties missing altogether from tax records.

Farm credit was also hard to come by, because of the tight banking regulations being enforced in those trying times. The Federal government did set a ceiling of eight per cent interest on bank loans; but some banks resorted to double dealing through loan company "fronts," which charged exorbitant rates.

B. V. Widney, Whitley county, for a long time a county agricultural agent, believes that area organized primarily to help facilitate the extension program for better farming and better homemaking . . . "and to prepare and promote constructive farm legislation at state and national levels. Some joined in the hope of correcting abuses of over-charging (for farm supplies) and under-paying (for commodities) by local merchants and dealers."

Ernest R. Schowe, Clark county, credits the sudden drop in 1920 farm prices with giving a boost to the early efforts to obtain members. I. H. Hull, LaPorte county farmer at the time but since a district Farm Bureau director and the first general manager of the Indiana Farm Bureau Co-operative Association, says: "Fear drove us together."

L. L. Needler, Shelby county, once a fourth district director of Farm Bureau, and later a department head of Indiana Farm Bureau, sensed a feeling among some farmers of being overwhelmed by government regulatory agencies during the War; and he believes farmers organized to hold their own with this growing bureaucracy in Washington and with the labor unions in cities.

In Ohio county, farmers had organized earlier than 1919 as The Farmers' Equity. The Grange in Dearborn county had set a good example of how to organize for Ohio, its neighbor, when it readied itself to start a Farm Bureau. There, the purchase of a carload of sugar just at the close of the War, when sugar had been rationed and was expensive, proved to be a popular move to get farmers interested in the power of co-operative action. Steuben county organized in 1919 with 900 members, and T. I. Ferris as president.

Chauncey Downey, a charter member of Morgan county, tells of his township organizing to buy binder twine and fertilizer, then "we looked into livestock markets and grain sales." August Burger, Du-

bois county, reports they brought down the price of
fertilizer by $7 a ton the first year Farm Bureau was
in action. Twine costs within a few months dropped
six to eight cents a pound, saving as much as
$150,000 in one harvest.

In Vanderburgh county, we are told, a group of
War buddies had been meeting for fellowship to
become later the nucleus of the county Farm Bureau.

Road financing was a hot issue in those days.
Townships had been paying their own road costs
with property taxes. Poor townships had poor roads.
Now it was proposed that roads be built and supported or maintained by a county tax to make them
more uniform. Early Farm Bureau leaders opposed
this plan because "it would penalize the progressive
township to the benefit of the less progressive." Does
this have a familiar ring?

Response to the call to organize varied according
to the emotional thermometer reading on the hottest
issue in a community. It is significant that each
farmer saw in the budding Farm Bureau the answer
to his own particular problem. And he expected
results quickly.

At a called meeting in Hamilton county, interest
ran so high that the Wild Opera House in Noblesville
was filled to capacity and many, many more stood
outside, unable to get into the hall, according to
Paul Wheeler, long active in both Farm Bureau and
the co-operative.

It may help the reader to grasp the difficulties

encountered in those days to recall that many roads were not only not paved, they were not even graveled. George W. Elliott, for twenty years director of the tenth Farm Bureau district, refers to the frequent aid one farmer had to give another before he could get his car out of the mud after a meeting as "one of the first acts of co-operation among farmers."

There was no rural electricity in those days, either. A farmer always went to his Farm Bureau meeting lantern in hand, more than likely polished to a turn by his devoted wife.

When asked what kind of program they put on at an early meeting, when there was no electricity, one member said:

"You'd be surprised. "There were clever people in every gathering. I remember one time, we jacked up the back wheel of a car, belted the wheel to a generator that was clamped onto a running board. That gave us the current to run the slide projector so the county agent could show his pictures that went along with his talk." Today, with the same degree of difficulty in staging a program, many would stay at home.

In another community in which a Delco salesman resided, they were fortunate to have him demonstrate an individual generating plant designed for a single farm. This provided lights and power for the projector.

The farmers on such occasions began to see what they were missing by not having electricity. These demonstrations may have helped them make up their minds about the need for the Rural Electric Membership Co-operatives.

Mrs. Benjamin Edmundson, Danville, whose late husband was a county Farm Bureau president and national pioneer in developing the soybean crop to major status and was often heard to say that he had two loves, Farm Bureau and the Presbyterian church, tells of an occasion at a Liberty township meeting, Hendricks county, when more people came than were expected. The hostesses made their own adaptation of the Biblical story of the five loaves and two fishes. The doughnuts were cut in half and everyone was served.

A Carroll county meeting in a schoolhouse found itself short of seats. The chairman suggested that each man bring his own bench next month. Hammers and saws were put to work and the seating capacity thereafter was adequate.

Rugged Individualism

As rural life in the early twenties lacked its refinements, so did man who had been born and bred close to the soil. But he had learned a valuable lesson from this proximity to nature.

Yes, he often went to town with mud on his boots. His syntax left something to be desired; but in the character of every good farmer was and is stamped the belief that honesty is the best policy. As the late Dr. George D. Scarseth, eminent agronomist and long-time friend of Farm Bureau, put it: "You can't cheat on nature."

So integrity had to make do when sophistication was lacking. This lack also often meant the absence of tact. Individual farmers were enthusiastic over the new farm organization and excited about its prospects, and frequently irritated businessmen by threatening (perhaps jokingly) to put them out of business when there was no such intent on the part of the organization. Farmers also irritated other farmers.

John Curry, Sullivan county farmer and former president of the Indiana Farm Bureau Co-operative Association, recalls an incident which demonstrates this. The county agent had come by unexpectedly to take him to a township Farm Bureau meeting. En route the agent admitted that he hadn't been able to find a speaker for the evening as he had promised, and that he (Mr. Curry) would have to pinch hit.

"I was unprepared and embarrassed, but I did manage to talk for a while. At the close of the meeting, the chairman said to the county agent, in Curry's presence: 'You promised to provide a speaker. Next time, we will expect you to do so.' "

In many instances, the new county Farm Bureau president was inexperienced in the ways of conducting a meeting and other duties of the office. Moreover, he was frightened by his new responsibility. His knees shook. One asked his county agent: "Won't you take over and run it? It will be all right with me."

When assured that the agent would sit beside him and help, the president managed to get through the evening's chore.

Often, without intent, the new farm organization would do things that irritated the business community. After World War I, during which horses were used in ground fighting, the nation found itself with a surplus of harness. The government offered it at bargain prices, and farmers jumped at the opportunity. It was suggested that orders be left with the county agent, in whose office the harness was displayed. This act incensed other harness dealers and brought down their wrath on the head of the hapless agent.

A school issue in one Carroll county township had so incensed the people that the peace and order of an approaching Farm Bureau meeting was threatened. The township president appealed to the county president, Sam Smith, to help him save the day. Smith was asked to provide speakers who would skirt the school issue, and some entertainment that would not allow time for the school argument to be revived.

Smith recalls the incident with amusement. Three Farm Bureau speakers were engaged who promised to talk only of organization achievements; and a group of musicians promised to come and play. Everything went off as planned, except that the entertainment proved so popular that the musicians received many encores. Geniality took over, and several new Farm Bureau members were enrolled.

Guy Cantwell recalls that during his three years as the first president of the Owen county Farm Bureau, he spent fifty days per year directly involved in work for the organization. He also reports that from the first the *county* was assured that it would be the governing unit in the Indiana Federation of Farmers' Associations. The first project in Owen county was a comparative study of property assessments for tax evaluation.

At the original meetings in townships and counties, few farmers had definite ideas about how to proceed or what to expect from this new giant they were creating. On one thing they were agreed. Their economic problems must come first.

But getting understanding across to farmers on all that was needed to make the organization successful was slow in coming, as any educational program must of necessity be slow. Limited knowledge was a stumbling block. The word "bureau" itself was confusing. Many thought it had something to do with the government.

Robert W. Curry, Monroe county charter member and long-time president of his county, remembers one elderly man, who when solicited for his membership, thought 'bureau' referred to a piece of bedroom furniture.

E. D. Blackmore of Greene county recalls early skepticism about what the organization would accomplish. "I don't believe it will do any good until it handles rakes, pitchforks, seeds and the like," one

man said. At that time, it was generally agreed that
the state organization would not try to replace the
middleman. Little did they guess that in a very short
time, the state organization would have a booming
co-operative that would offer stiff competition to the
middleman. But at first, farmers were very reluctant
to compete with small town businessmen,—their
neighbors.

We relate these glimpses of early activity at the
local level, because that is where it all began. The
organization rose from a deep, underlying desire of
the farmer to lift himself from the economic quag-
mire into which he was slipping. He yearned for
better things for himself and his family which he saw
others enjoying. These stirrings built into a virtual
ground swell which gave birth to the state federation. And action then, as now, started at the local
level.

Federation Is Born

It remained only for persons of sufficient stature
and leadership ability to weld this large body into
a more or less homogeneous whole to represent the
thinking of the farmers of the state, men bent on
helping themselves and their neighbors out of their
predicament.

Old records show that two "agitators" were in the
state before 1919 trying to organize farmers. The
fact they were regarded as agitators indicates they
were suspect. They were believed to have been from

the U.S. Department of Agriculture. However, the two men stayed on after the Federation was formed and trained leaders at regional meetings in the art of soliciting members and in parliamentary procedure.

One of the first effective moves to organize Farm Bureau came from Purdue leaders, Dean J. H. Skinner, T. A. Coleman, and Prof. W. C. Latta. They were prominent in a meeting called at Purdue in January, 1919, to start the ball rolling. Dean Skinner sounded the clarion call: "It is important that we get together in such a way as to have a voice in the big affairs which are going to take place in this country in the near future."

Perhaps the University Extension personnel can be forgiven for their selfish interests in a farm organization. Frankly, they needed it for getting new farming information to the men in the fields. They probably did not anticipate that it would become a strong, independent policy-making body. There is evidence some of them did not want it to become such.

But the basic purpose conceived by the leaders in the new organization soon began to crystallize. Lewis Taylor, first Federation general secretary, said at an early state organization meeting: "We want to understand our own business as thoroughly and completely as the meat packers understand their own,—and ours, too, for that matter. We should have a man in the Argentine . . . if we are to compete with the South America republic . . . we should also have experts in Europe to give us first-hand information."

This proclamation was partially prophetic, since now, fifty years later, the American Farm Bureau Federation does employ men who are selling American agricultural products in foreign trade. Among these early leaders, there was often an uncanny sense of the future in what they said and did.

At the January meeting, discontent over dropping farm prices came out in the open. The crisis a-building served as a goad to the efforts to organize. In less troubled times, it would have been more difficult.

A committee was named to arrange a state meeting to be held in Indianapolis in February. Things were moving rapidly. On that committee were: Dr. C. W. Hickman, M.D. turned farmer from Tippecanoe county; Milton Reiff, White county; E. E. Reynolds, Tippecanoe county; W. F. Franklin, Hendricks county; and Frank J. Goodwin, Warren county.

At the February gathering, there were forty present from fifteen counties. On that occasion, it was decided to send someone into the counties to survey farmer feeling about the effort to organize. Since Mr. Franklin had spoken at some length on this subject, he was tapped for the dubious honor of making the survey,—dubious because of its monumental proportions. For this work, he has since been considered the first organization director of the Indiana Farm Bureau.

At the February meeting Franklin also clarified the relationship which he believed should exist between the organization and Purdue University. As an enthusiastic friend of Purdue, he appreciated the excellent work it had done, and felt sure that both the University and the Extension Service would co-operate fully with the farmers' federation.

"The limitation on the kinds of work they are allowed by law to do is spelled out in the Vocational Education Law of 1913," he explained. "They should not be asked to participate in commercial activity."

Others speaking out at this early meeting were: Edwood Morris, Hancock county; J. W. Keefer, Kosciusko; Jonathan Lowe, Hendricks; L. G. Vannice, Hendricks; H. D. Coombs, Montgomery; Dr. C. W. Hickman, Tippecanoe; O. L. Mitchell, Boone; Dr. C. H. Smith, Lake; W. J. Lawson, Benton; and Dr. E. T. Davis, Hendricks.

The challenge which faced the Hickman committee was that of bringing into existence the organization which they envisioned. Farmers' acceptance could not yet be taken for granted.

Hickman, Franklin, and Lawson were asked to draw up a constitution and by-laws to present at a statewide meeting of farmers to be held March 25, 1919.

The organizers had established state headquarters in Room 369 of the old English Hotel on the northwest segment of the Circle in Indianapolis. The March event was held in the Claypool, but the evening before that significant day the English lobby buzzed with farm talk and organization politics.

Among those gathered there were the original leaders of the body that was to become an agricultural institution.

This new body was to be called The Indiana Federation of Farmers' Associations. In the name itself one can sense the reluctance members felt toward a potential state organization that might jeopardize their liberty. This sentiment was to show up time and again in the development of what was later to be known as the Indiana Farm Bureau.

It was the same reluctance which resulted in the late eighteenth century American Confederation of states, and with the same grief. They met the same problems. Both had to be strengthened at the top to make them effective instruments in achieving their avowed purposes. The move toward a stronger farm organization followed, once members gained confidence in the leadership.

The ghost of the violence and disruption of war hovered over every move and every problem and every policy developed to solve that problem in those early days. It had upset the farm economy and drained away thousands and thousands of farm boys who returned to go into the city to work. It shaped and colored every Farm Bureau gathering.

At the November 15, 1920, state convention a Mr. Sims of Daviess County presented the Federation

with a gavel made from a broken flagstaff of Battery
E, Seventh Field Artillery, that was broken during
the Battle of the Argonne Forest in World War I.

Lewis Taylor, named chairman of the March
meeting, had this to say in the patriotic tenor of the
day: "We must try to solve these questions with a
sense of justice to all concerned, if we are to live
as an organized body of farmers . . . and I want to
say our deliberations today should show to the world
that to the farmers, the red flag is intolerable; and
that now, as ever before, the farmer is to take counsel
from the lips of Washington, Jefferson, Lincoln and
Roosevelt (T.R.) as they speak to us from every
fiber of our incomparable banner—the red, white
and blue."

Stirring words, these. While spoken soon after the
close of the war, when every gathering could be expected to voice some patriotic sentiment, it is rather
unusual that at this juncture of our history, a farm
leader sensed the danger of Bolshevism which was
stirring up unrest in Russia.

Discussion at the March meeting became heated.
There were threatening differences of opinion on
how the Federation was to be administered. Voices
rose. There was some table pounding, then a calm
voice (that of Kosciusko's Mr. Keefer) penetrated
the discord and asked that "this body stop for prayer
so that we may return to our labors with order and
sanity."

The incident had a sobering influence on the years that were to follow. To this day, Farm Bureau meetings open with prayer. Despite the travail that developed there, the state organization was born on that day, March 25, 1919. Three days after this meeting, Henry county joined the state federation to become the first in Indiana to do so. Since there was a great deal of work to be done, state meetings were held almost monthly during that first year.

At an April meeting in Indianapolis, it was decided that Indiana should be divided into ten districts, with one director per district. These directors, together with the state officers, would constitute the state board of directors. It was also agreed that only those counties which had organized could be represented by delegates at the first state convention set for November. Amazingly enough, like mushrooms in springtime, fifty-four counties had done so before the gavel opened that first momentous occasion on November 18.

The April session also issued a declaration of principles. Unschooled in the ways of organization, these farmers were proving their abilities and rising to their new responsibilities. What they said in that declaration is particularly significant. Three reasons for their organizing were:

1. For mutual protection as any other class of workers and producers; (regarding themselves as both laborers and businessmen)

2. To promote farm home betterment and the general interest and welfare of communities;

3. To preserve and extend our civil and religious institutions.

As general policy, they also stated: "We shall stand for law and order . . . The farmers of Indiana will not go to extremes. We have farmers smarting under the wrongs we have suffered all these years, but they will not seek correction in wrong ways, or extreme ways to right wrongs."

Time and again they stressed they were "not Bolshevik."

By way of action, the meeting recorded: "We therefore call for legislation from the U.S. Congress . . . to stabilize prices of food products." The proceedings were signed by the first board of directors, officers and others, one of whom was Earl Crawford, a Wayne county farmer who was also, at the time, a member of the Indiana State Highway Commission.

Listed in the order of their districts, starting with the first, the original directors were: J. A. Warren, Porter county; Hugh M. Widney, St. Joseph; Dr. C. W. Hickman, Tippecanoe; H. T. Walker, Blackford; W. F. Franklin, Hendricks; F. P. Mullens, Madison; V. D. Sexton, Green; L. M. Vogler, Bartholomew; John J. Brown, Spencer; and John G. Klein, Ripley.

These men dreamed no small dreams. In an early issue of The HOOSIER FARMER, Dr. Hickman envisioned "a great agricultural temple in Indian-

apolis with a publishing department and an auditorium." This dream was in part realized later in
the acquisition of a printing plant in Spencer,
Indiana. Later also, two downtown office buildings
in Indianapolis were purchased to house state Farm
Bureau headquarters, the home office of Farm Bureau Insurance Companies, and headquarters for
Indiana Farm Bureau Co-operative Association.
While these buildings are not strictly speaking agricultural temples, they are valuable pieces of property owned by farmers of Indiana.

Political leaders were quick to see the potential
influence of this young farm giant lumbering into
action in 1919. Governor James P. Goodrich, speaking before a gathering of farmers, said: "You don't
know, men, how it strengthens the arm of public
officials . . . to know that they have behind them
the best sentiment in the state." This may have been
political opportunism at work, or it may have been a
sincere expression. It must be remembered that at
that time there were 218,000 farms in Indiana, a
number to be reckoned with in any election.

By July, state Federation leaders were painfully
aware of the need for money to operate the ambitious
program which was in the making. The individual
farmer did not share that awareness, and so had to
be sold on the great need for a substantial treasury.

State leaders at this time asked that each county
contribute $200 to finance the Federation's program.
They boldly stated they needed $200,000 which

seemed like a vast sum to most farmers but which later proved much too small to support the extensive purpose of the Federation.

Membership in the Better Farming Associations had been free or had required only an occasional small assessment to cover a current local need. It was difficult for members of the new state organization to grasp the urgency for a fixed and dependable income.

The program from the beginning was comprehensive, though poorly planned at first. When the organization workers went into the counties, they took with them no uniformity of plan or fixed dues to be asked. Consequently, some counties levied as little as fifty cents per year, while others started with a ten-dollar membership fee.

Some drew up a three-to-five-year agreement at a fixed fee per year. This plan served to carry over a member from one year to the next, though many defaulted when money became scarce.

At a state meeting in July, it was proposed (rather presumptuously it seems in retrospect) that every farm be assessed one-fourth mill per hundred dollars on its taxable valuation, or one dollar per farm, whichever was larger. This was to be paid whether or not the owner belonged to Farm Bureau. This plan was defended by the statement: "This is a movement of all farmers for the benefit of all farmers."

It is not recorded whether this suggestion was successful in any degree, but Farm Bureau had no real power to collect the assessment.

At the same time the Indiana Farmers' Federation was wrestling with its financial foundation, Ohio, Michigan, Kentucky and Iowa had already established a ten-dollar membership fee, and Illinois had gone to fifteen dollars.

In May, 1919, Madison, Shelby and Rush counties had started their membership drive with a five-dollar fee and already had among the largest enrollments in the state—staunch argument against those who said that farmers would not pay that much.

Ernest R. Schowe of Clark county recalls that one farmer, who contributed five dollars to get the organization started, refused to join later because he thought his "donation" was all that would ever be asked of him.

Hassil E. Schenck, fourth president of the Indiana Farm Bureau, was a struggling, young farmer in Boone county when the organization saw its inception. When he was approached to join, he was understandably hesitant.

"Dollars were as big as cartwheels in those days," he laughs. "I think quite often of the arguments I resorted to, to show why I should not obligate myself for twenty-five dollars over a period of five years." This was the plan followed in his county at the beginning. Wallace Ross takes pride in the fact that it was he who persuaded Mr. Schenck to join.

I. H. Hull, who had come to LaPorte county from Illinois, helped in the first county-wide drive for members. Going along with him were M. J. Briggs, at that time a Miami county farmer and later to become general manager of the Indiana Farm Bureau Co-operative Association, and County Agent C. A. Beuchner—Both lovers of Dutch Masters cigars. Hull offered to buy a box of cigars every time they succeeded in signing up one hundred per cent of the farmers in a township.

The men enrolled 1,785 for three years, and the effort cost Hull five boxes of "smokes." The county organization was so grateful, it later repaid Hull in full.

Elmer Jacks of Jasper county recalls soliciting members in towns and sometimes finding businessmen more receptive than were farmers. "They could see that if the farmer didn't prosper, they wouldn't either," he concludes.

In Montgomery county, dues were first set at one dollar per year, and at the end of the first year there were 2,000 members.

Frank Beall, at one time president of the Indiana Farm Bureau Co-operative Association and later employed by that organization to launch a program of education, public relations and personnel orientation, believes there were more members in his native Decatur county in those first years than they now have, largely because there were more farmers then.

Chester Clark of Lake county avers that one of the greatest boosts to membership in that part of

the state was a remark by a state representative from
Whiting, who told farmers when they sought his
help: "You go home and do your farming. We'll
run the legislature."

This sort of condescension was frequently voiced,
but it actually served as the goad the farmers needed.

They came out fighting.

But all was not solved when a farmer agreed to
join the Federation. He, as well as state leaders, expected great things to happen quickly, though initial
efforts were poorly organized, all-encompassing and
too often ineffectual. There were farm problems to
be solved and organization problems to be righted;
but big problems do not give way quickly.

Eighty-one of the ninety-two counties had organized by the end of 1919. A year later there were
64,420 members in the state. Then the tide began
to turn.

The leaders saw they would have to engage in
commercial activity if they were to have any influence on the prices of things they had to buy or sell.
This was apparent despite the fact that many counties
had gone on record saying they would not engage
in such ventures. But farmers needed leverage of
some kind over the prices they were forced to pay
for their supplies, and bargaining strength if they
were to get better prices for their products.

Some local groups had started by buying carloads
of fertilizer, coal, binder twine and even sugar. Some
of these enterprises had been complicated by hard-

ened fertilizer and knotty twine. Local businessmen in the farm supply business capitalized on farm discontent which arose over this poor quality.

Carping from the Gallery

While criticism from outsiders against Farm Bureau activities, and even at first against its very reason for existence, had been almost negligible, some of it is worth analyzing. When membership solicitors uttered threatening or disparaging remarks about businessmen, the organization reaped the criticism it deserved. In some areas, however, there was complete acceptance, one of the other, in the community and businessmen were among the first to join.

There was a time when the laboring man's grievance against the high cost of living (this was before the days when the escalator clause was written into his contract) was leveled at farmers whom they accused of profiteering in food.

Criticism came also from another farm publication when The ORGANIZED FARMER (the first name adopted for the official Federation magazine) appeared in the mails. The other publication, then known as The Indiana Farmer's Guide, perhaps saw a threat to its own existence—a threat never intended by the magazine nor its sponsor.

In the exchange of charge and counter charge between the editors of the two publications, one statement appeared in The HOOSIER FARMER Organized, the magazine name adopted in August,

1919 by the Federation, which indicates there may have been overtures by The Guide in the hope it would become the voice of the new farm organization. The statement read, in defense of something Lewis Taylor, then secretary, is supposed to have said in public:

"Taylor had said: 'What we all had said is that we could not expect any paper to become our official organ whose editorial policy we could not control!' A number of papers had sought to become our official organ."

The Guide editor warned farmers they should investigate the way in which their money was being spent in the state Federation. It was also charged that the new organization was not being run by farmers.

The latter charge was in part true. There were some men active in the formative months whose primary interest was not agriculture. Their incomes were from real estate, insurance, funeral directing and other endeavors. Some of the early leaders had been school teachers or physicians, turned farmers but farmers nonetheless. One can only guess what businessmen hoped to gain from helping the farmers organize, beyond their civic interest in community betterment.

After a few short years and after the board of directors in 1921 had amended the by-laws, bona fide farmers took full control.

After it was demonstrated to The Guide that the two publications could exist side by side in Indiana, strained relations were turned into a most affable working relationship. As the Farm Bureau program expanded to include the good of the entire community and demonstrated that the organization had no ulterior motive against any group or economic segment, opposition began to subside.

Richard Graves, Fulton county farmer, who participated in the march of 10,000 farmers to the State House in 1939 on invitation of the Governor to prevent repeal of the Gross Income Tax, recalls some ridicule from the sidelines as they headed for the state capitol. Some onlookers (he imagines they were packers) squealed like pigs and mooed like cows to deride this demonstration of farmer interest in government.

After the subsequent hearing, the crowd retreated and the same onlookers were heard to say: "Let's go home; we're licked."

There were frequent accusations that farmers were sticking their noses into others' affairs. Frank Beall recalls a businessman saying: "It's all right for farmers to get together to eat sandwiches and drink coffee, but they ought not to get into civic affairs. One township assessor nearly choked when we upset his unfair assessment by appealing to the County Board of Review."

Some of the opposition was covert. One such effort came when farmers were trying to organize to regulate the selling of grain more to their own advantage, rather than only to the advantage of the handlers. This came at a time when the market co-operated with the handlers, and farmers became distrustful of their own leaders. Whether the market was actually manipulated to bring about the fiasco is not known, but the result was what the dealers wanted.

Southern Indiana tobacco growers had a friend in Robert W. Bingham, Louisville, Kentucky, newspaper publisher, who characterized the Federation critics and explained their motives by writing: "Their graft is being cut off."

In more recent years, farmer-owned co-operatives have come under fire, principally from the National Tax Equality Association, because of the exemption of some co-operatives from the federal net income tax. The Association filled the mails in a concerted drive to discredit the farm co-ops. It charged special privilege, called them "big business" and indulged in other such half-truths. The Association failed to mention the fact that the co-operatives were complying with federal law—a law which also exempts mutual associations and other profit-sharing enterprises. This flurry, too, in time died down.

Farm Bureau and Purdue

From such areas as the Land Grant College and the Co-operative Extension Service, one could rightfully expect support for the new farm organization. Even here, however, there were differences of opinion about the final role Farm Bureau was to play. People may think they are moving in the same direction, but it often develops they have their eyes on different goals and so must eventually take a different fork in the road.

Although the Extension Service had by Act of Congress been established some ten years before the Indiana Federation of Farmers' Associations came into being, it was not to be fully implemented for many years. It remained for the counties to establish financial support for the program. The county board of education by state law had to approve of the candidate for the county agent's job before he could be employed. The agent was at first hired for one year at a time—a precarious situation at best. Moreover, in 1919 federal money for each agent was reduced from $1,080 to $240 per year.

The board of education was comprised of the township trustees and the county superintendent of schools. Not all of them could be expected to be eager to spend money for the benefit of farmers. They did not immediately see that an improved rural economy would reflect to the general good.

L. E. Hoffman, whose life work in the Extension Service paralleled that of the Indiana Farm Bureau until his retirement in 1962, relates some of the amusing and what must have been harassing circumstances in the beginning years of Extension work

when the program's continuance depended a great
deal on Farm Bureau help.

When Mr. Hoffman was assistant supervisor of
county agents, he was sent to Dubois county to try
to persuade officials there to hire an agricultural
agent. William Gentry, president of the county Farm
Bureau, was earnestly seeking the education board's
approval of an agent, whose services Gentry was
convinced the community needed.

The meeting was called for 10:30 a.m. It was
soon apparent there were more against than for the
proposition. Hoffman managed to extend the discussion until after lunch to allow time for some "poli-
ticking." After lunch the meeting resumed and did
vote to employ the agent. Gentry was so elated, he
beamed: "I must go home to tell Mama."

As Hoffman's next point of call was Evansville,
he immediately took the train southward. As the
cars clicked over the steel rails through the countryside, Hoffman noticed a horse and rider keeping
pace with the locomotive. Lickety-split, the horse
obviously enjoying it, the man now identified as
Gentry, waving his arms with joy as he hurried "home
to tell Mama."

On many similar occasions, Farm Bureau worked
diligently to get the extension program going. The
money for it had to be budgeted by the County Commissioners, appropriated by the County Council, and
the applicant for the position of county agent had to
be approved by the board of education. A great deal

of persuasion and influence were employed by Farm Bureau members at the local level.

Often Farm Bureau donated money to mete out the Council's appropriation. In 1911, the Indiana General Assembly made a token appropriation for Extension work in Indiana. A 1913 permissive Act allowed counties to appropriate money to implement the program, but it was still not mandatory. From that year until 1937, when a mandatory measure did become law, Extension leaders were counstantly faced with the problem of getting counties to hire agents, for without them the service could not function.

This is the period during which Farm Bureau was of real help. Once the organization was formed, farmer influence with county officials carried more weight.

In a sense, Purdue Extension Service and Farm Bureau complemented each other. Some counties went on record in their original statement of purpose as intending to work closely with the Land Grant College and Extension Service. Such a county was Hendricks, which stated as early as February, 1919: "While this is purely a farmers' organization, and will be organized and run by farmers, it is not the purpose to divorce themselves from the agricultural college nor the county agents."

From the beginning, Purdue agricultural administrators saw in the new Federation a ready-made instrument for the extension program. There were farmers who sincerely believed that such an attachment would limit the true function of the organization. Others argued that they needed to work closely with the Land Grant College and that no harm could come of it.

Early organization politics felt this difference of viewpoint. But the infant was not long to stay in its mother's arms once it had outgrown the swaddling clothes. It had work to do, over and beyond the learning of better farming methods which the extension program offered.

Like many parents emotionally torn when the children leave home, University agricultural leaders, according to some who were active in those days, were hurt when they realized they could no longer direct the Farm Bureau course.

Several years were to pass before a sound and pleasant working relationship would be restored. Everyone now seems happy with the results. When one considers the fact that a few years ago the Federal government issued an ultimatum of severance of any farm organization from the Land Grant Colleges and Extension Service, he can appreciate the early struggle which effected the same end in Indiana. Some states felt a distinct wrench in their Farm Bureau organizational structure when this government edict had to be carried out.

Independently, Farm Bureau continues to support the Extension program. It has, over the years, given scholarships to the winter short course for young farmers. It worked for several years to secure enactment of a permissive law and supporting funds to establish a School of Veterinary Medicine at Purdue. While this new School benefits farmers through more trained veterinarians, it also adds to the University's status.

Farm Bureau was also active in the establishment of a Swine Evaluation Station at Purdue. Farm Bureau personnel, with the help of the Producers Marketing Association, aided in the development of the meat-type hog, with Purdue scientists conducting the studies and making the results public. A certification program carried on at the Station promises to upgrade permanently the Indiana swine industry, thus making available the quality pork demanded by today's consumer.

Farm Bureau was called upon several years ago to solicit funds in southern Indiana for purchasing acreage in Dubois county for Purdue to conduct forage experiments. The success of this effort will be measured in increased income for farmers in that part of the state, as well as elsewhere.

The Indiana Farm Bureau and affiliates joined in a ten-year venture in support of Purdue research in improving varieties of alfalfa, drying and storage methods, comparative nutritional properties, and in developing strains resistant to disease. During this period the Farm Bureau family contributed $120,-000 to these experiments and studies, considered a definite success.

In 1963 another alfalfa project was launched for a three-year period to develop a creeping type plant that will withstand heaving in cold weather, particularly in southern Indiana where this occurs more often than in the colder northern section. This project required $4,500 per year, $1,500 of which came from Indiana Farm Bureau and the remainder from affiliates and the Production Credit Associations of Indiana.

In rural youth educational work, Farm Bureau has been the right hand of Extension Service. State agricultural leaders saw that any program starts best with young people. Boys' and girls' 4-H clubs were organized to stimulate interest in better farming methods. Farm Bureau has, through the years, provided adult sponsors and junior leaders from among its member families.

The results have been two-fold. The youngsters were given constructive work to do during the summer months, and fathers learned from their children's demonstrations. Also, these boys and girls often provided entertainment at the local Farm Bureau meeting, and parents who came alone became interested in Farm Bureau and decided to join.

In the late thirties, Extension leaders observed that some rural youth beyond high school and not yet married nor attending college were social drifters. They were too old to be interested in children's activities, and too young to join fully adult groups.

In 1938 a state federation of rural youth was formed under the name of Indiana Rural Youth, with county clubs as the basic units. This organization includes youth from 18 to 30 years of age. More recently the clubs also welcome into membership rural youth who have gone to towns and cities to work.

These clubs are co-sponsored by Purdue Extension and Farm Bureau. The county Bureaus provide adult advisers to work with the local Rural Youth. Unnumbered hours have been spent in guiding these young people in their community programs.

These clubs also investigate and get instruction about available opportunities for work. They study current problems and functions of government. They are encouraged in the habits of good health through right living and wholesome recreation. Members serve as volunteers in community drives for charity and public welfare.

From Indiana Rural Youth have come many Farm Bureau leaders. One of the most outstanding among these is George Doup, incumbent president of Indiana Farm Bureau, who was the first president of Indiana Rural Youth.

The Marthas and the Marys

When Shakespeare wrote "Frailty, thy name is woman," he revealed that his acquaintance was limited to the ladies of the British Royal Court and the theater at which he worked. He did not know

Indiana farm women, the Marthas and the Marys who complement their husbands' activities in operating their farms, who lend grace and gentility to the farm home; who cook and bake, and at times cultivate; who make speeches in public places; who sew and mend and guide their children "in the ways of righteousness."

It was such as these who came to be and remain an integral part of the Indiana Farm Bureau. One wonders how they found the energy to do more than they were already doing, for the life of a farm woman in the early twenties was indeed arduous.

Miss Lella Gaddis, first state leader of home demonstration work through the Extension program, is quoted as having said: "It took a lot of nerve (in those days) for a young man to ask his young woman to marry him and carry a barrel of water every day." That task actually faced every farm woman if she hoped to run her houshold in satisfactory fashion. We can be glad there were few faint hearts.

As Farm Bureau developed, conditions for the farm woman were inordinately trying. It has always been woman who must adjust family living expenses to income. Woman's versatility in the twenties and thirties was severely put to the test. Pages of The HOOSIER FARMER in an early issue instructed women in the art of canning spareribs, and in making over an old dress. Today she may be told how to make a souffle or a party dress.

When the Indiana Federation of Farmers' Associations was formed women were not immediately admitted. They often accompanied their husbands to a meeting, but waited outside in the buggy, sometimes even when the weather was cold. More often they stopped at a neighbor's home to spend the evening.

It is recalled by these pioneer women that so long as women were not invited to join in the meeting, the men came unshaven and often clad in their work clothes.

While women were theoretically admitted to membership as early as September, 1919, their participation did not actually take shape until two years later. There were several reasons for this. Farmers psychologically were especially backward in according equal rights to women. It was not until 1920, with passage of the Nineteenth Amendment to the U.S. Constitution, that women were given the right to vote. Many men were reluctant for some time after that to grant equal status to women.

Token acceptance of woman's role in the new farm organization was made in such early statements as: "We hope it may be generally known that women have the same rights and privileges to membership in the Federation of Farmers' Association as men. There are great fields now open for the work of woman . . . We are planning to take up sanitation and other helpful activities to promote and protect the farm home and community . . . Women are urged to join the Federation on the same terms as men, as we need their help and they need the help of men in this great co-operative movement."

This was first president, John G. Brown, speaking. It remained for him to get the women's program rolling. One of his first concerns was the low quality of rural schools.

On March 6, 1922, he called a state meeting to outline a program for women in the Federation. At the time there were many township and county organizations not yet ready to accept women. For this reason, much of the original instigation had to come from the top of the organizational structure.

It was at first proposed that the women's program be financed by separate dues. When there was already one membership in the family, the woman was to pay $1.50 per year; if not, she was to pay $2.

The woman's program, materialized in what was at first called the Social and Educational Department, was directed by a man—L. A. Pittenger of Delaware county, sixth district director of the state organization. This selection is understandable. Mr. Pittenger, who had been a teacher who turned to farming on his doctor's advice, later returned to teaching and became president of what is now Ball State University. Since one of President Brown's primary interests was the improvement of rural schools, it was only natural for him to turn to the man who was most familiar with the problem, as the person best fitted to initiate the women's program with an emphasis on rural school improvement.

The scope of women's activities grew rapidly. At the March meeting, the women were told they "would hold up a mirror to the agricultural genius of the state." We assume this started the search for rural talent, which in the years since has discovered and encouraged the abilities of both young and old. This effort has sent entertainers to the Indiana State Fair, some to continue on to national competition. Women have also assisted with boys' and girls' club work. They have helped develop leaders not only for Farm Bureau activities but also to participate in the civic growth of hundreds of Indiana communities.

Mrs. Charles W. Sewell of Benton county was chairman of that March, '22, meeting. Those present spoke out for better homes, better schools, and a more rich and varied life for adult and youth. *They asked that farming be elevated beyond sowing and reaping and profit.* This Benton county farm woman, who in 1925 became the first woman elected to the Indiana Farm Bureau board of directors, later was named head of the women's department and then chairman of home and community activities of the American Farm Bureau Federation for 16 years, spelled out her philosophy in these words: "You can't be loyal indefinitely to a fertilizer bag, an oil drum or an insurance policy."

This insight, common to women in Farm Bureau (and perhaps to women generally) is their most significant contribution to Farm Bureau's growth and stability. They have injected moral and spiritual values where men might be primarily concerned with the market place.

Although the early program inaugurated by women under the Social and Educational Department is reputed to have been "not very social" and "not very educational" it did lead to real achievement. The women were undaunted. Soon, evidence of their good works was everywhere.

President Brown appointed an advisory committee from among those present at that March meeting. Besides Mrs. Sewell, they were: Miss Anna Mohnssen, Porter county; Mesdames Nora Favinger, Noble; C. E. Moseley, Miami; Lawrence Foster, Montgomery; Lillian T. Pierce, Henry; E. H. Baker, Martin; M. P. Jones, Union; C. N. Lindley, Washington; and Lewis Taylor, Warrick.

The women's program, however, did not seem to "jell." Many women's groups held separate meetings. Complete merger with the Farm Bureau program, with the women as a part of the family membership, did not occur for several years.

Today there are township, county and district woman leaders, township and county Pet and Hobby Club leaders, women members of important Farm Bureau committees, and some women secretaries and treasurers at different levels of the organization. Some are content and effective playing the traditional role of woman. They plan the details of the program for the Farm Bureau meeting, set the table before the crowd arrives, and provide the food that has been

credited by some as the only reason people come to
the meeting; but praised by others as contributing
to an atmosphere of neighborliness.

On February 3, 1923, the S. and E. Committee
composed of ten appointed district woman leaders,
met in Indianapolis and outlined a more extensive
and definitive program. Mr. Pittenger, as women's
department head, was present. At this time, the new
president, William H. Settle, Wells county, appointed Mrs. Ed (Verna) Hatch of Allen county
as chairman of the women. It was not until three
years later that Mrs. Hatch was considered the department head.

Joining her on a new planning committee were
Mrs. Lindley and Mrs. Foster. These women recog-

nized their program must fit the needs of the individual community; that it must remain flexible if it were to be adaptable. Before public relations had become a part of the Farm Bureau program, these women showed rare foresight in admitting they had to have a good publicity plan. This was especially true, because their first order of business was to "sell" the women's program to a hundred thousand farm women in the state.

They also recommended that two-day schools be conducted by the state organization in such practical matters as wool grading and marketing, other product grading, grain standardization, better livestock shipping conditions, and in organization membership work. These women had apparently been listening to man talk and were quick to recognize that where the farm business was at stake, so was their family's standard of living.

The district leaders were advised to go home and appoint township and county women leaders. It was not possible to elect them democratically at that time, because there was not enough participation by women.

In helping plan the local meeting, women often resorted to the dramatic skit to put across an idea. One such skit was staged at an early state convention. Mrs. Sewell, who was assisted by others, considered that effort as one of her early triumphs. It was a mock wedding with such 'sinister' influences as the Board of Trade and Purdue University represented by glamorous young men lurking along the aisle, each trying to win the bride from her farmer bridegroom. This little drama can be understood when one realizes that it occurred at a time when Farm Bureau was learning to stand on its own feet, and also when the Board of Trade was being suspected of profiteering on grain at the farmer's expense.

Farm Bureau women were also asked to provide entertainment for women attending the National Dairy Show in Indianapolis. This gave them experience and status at state and national levels. They also helped to establish the Indiana State Fair Girls' Camp, an experience in working and living together for outstanding 4-H girls from all parts of the state.

The county Federation paid the expenses of one girl to this ten-day Camp, but not for nothing in return. The girl chosen was the one who had obtained the largest number of Federation members. This practice has since been dropped, but the Camp is still held annually, immediately prior to the opening of the Fair.

On almost any July Sunday (sometimes on a week-day) women in Farm Bureau may be seen, a towering, frosted cake in hand and/or ushering the little ones in their summer togs to a nearby park for the annual county picnic. On these occasions, a cake baking contest may be the height of the day for the women; or their children, nervous as sparrows, will compete in the amateur talent contest for the right to perform at the State Fair, and in so doing

arouse a tingling pride that only mothers can experience. Sometimes children will bring bouquets of
zinnias clutched too tightly in their inexperienced
hands. The flower show that follows is one of the
projects sponsored for many years by the Indiana
Farm Bureau Co-operative Association to encourage
children in beautifying their homes. The flowers are
grown by the children and prizes are given for the
best displays. The summer picnic is the one traditional event during the Farm Bureau year that is
primarily a social affair, any attempt by a scheduled
speaker notwithstanding.

Mrs. Pearl Mabbitt of Carroll county likes to
recall one picnic when the women agreed to wear
old-fashioned costumes. "Mine had been worn at
some big government function in Washington," she
says.

Indiana organization workers today will admit
that where women are active in the local Farm
Bureau, there you will find a vigorous, aggressive
and going concern. While the women's program has
expanded from purely local interests to state, national and international affairs, its greatest contribution has come at the local level. Expanded horizons
have served to keep them informed and better able
to understand current farm issues. As Mrs. Andrew
Metheny, former woman leader of Marshall county,
observed: "I preferred Farm Bureau work to other
women's organizations because it opened up wider
horizons."

Former State Woman Leaders

Verna Hatch
1926-1928

Gertrude Modlin
1928-1929

Edna Sewell
1929-1935

Lillie D. Scott
1935-1947

Ethel Cushman
1947-1955

Nellie Flinn
1955-1957

District Farm Bureau Woman Leaders (1968) are (left to right) standing: Mrs. Albert Schwiersch, Evansville; Mrs. Glendon Herbert, Cloverdale; Mrs. Arthur Etchison, Elwood; Mrs. James Viney, Monticello; and Mrs. James Hon, Florence. (Seated are): Mrs. Pearl Fidler, Sullivan; Mrs. Edwin G. Olson, Winamac; Mrs. Guy E. Gross, Churubusco, state woman leader, and second vice president, IFB; Mrs. George Felger, Churubusco; Mrs. Carl Myers, Petroleum; and Mrs. Webster Heck, Connersville.

(At right): Hancock county FB woman leaders gather at one of their homes to make Farm Bureau flag. 1934.

(Above): FB co-sponsors Indiana Rural Youth (young people between 18 and 28) with the Cooperative Extension Service. This float appeared in the Farmers' Day Parade at the State Fair.

(Below): Pet and Hobby clubs for farm youngsters under 10 years of age are sponsored by FB. These young people are parading their pets at the State Fair.

(Above): State officers of Indiana Future Farmers meet with FB Vice-president (seated, right) and other FB officials each year. FB sponsors several FFA awards.

(Below): The Indiana Youthpower Conference brings more than 100 leaders of 15 youth organizations together for a two-day discussion of food, nutrition, and other subjects of interest to young people. FB is an active sponsor.

These women have come a long way. At the first annual convention of the Indiana Farm Bureau, only three wives were present: Mrs. Lewis Taylor and Mrs. E. E. Reynolds, Tippecanoe county, both of whose husbands were state officers; and Mrs. William Brookshire, Henry county.

At the second annual convention of the American Farm Bureau Federation, held in Indianapolis, December, 1920, an Indiana woman was to make an unusual debut which would launch her into national prominence.

When national officers arrived for the event, they learned that one of their key speakers, Sir Aukland Geddes, British ambassador to the United States, had sent his regrets. His coming had been widely publicized. It was an awkward situation. Anyone of great importance would be offended if he were asked to substitute at so late an hour.

After a hasty conference, an Indiana leader said: "We have a woman if she can come."

That woman, Mrs. Sewell, said she had been reading about the convention and wishing that she could attend, "but money was scarce." It was a Monday morning, and this typical Hoosier homemaker had the weekly washing well under way. She had planned to churn "a couple of gallons of cream that were ripening in the milk box, which served as a refrigerator." And since it was only a few weeks before Christmas, she had also planned to bake a fruit cake.

"I had made good progress with the wash when the phone rang," she recalls. "When I answered, I heard the familiar clicks of other receivers on the party line."

The call was from Maurice Douglas, the state organization's second vice-president, who explained their predicament.

"Would I come and speak? Here I was washing, and it was less than three hours till train time at Otterbein five miles away. Maurice was confident that I would come, and with some breezy instructions on where and when to report upon my arrival, he hung up," she reported.

History records that this Indiana farm woman received a standing ovation when she finished her address; and before she returned home she had agreed to speak in a number of other states and in Lake county, Indiana, the coming Saturday night.

This is the kind of adaptability that served Mrs. Sewell well in a national capacity later. Other Indiana women have found themselves in demanding situations, where loyalty to the organization has exacted from them more imagination and energy than they suspected they had. These woman leaders have driven literally thousands of miles to help interpret Farm Bureau to other people, especially to the younger generation who are not familiar with the full story, and to give encouragement to those loyal volunteer leaders in the local units.

Today's program, as conceived and directed by Farm Bureau women is very comprehensive. They sponsor an extensive awards program, some of which is financially supported by the Farm Bureau insurance companies. They offer prizes to winners in public speaking in two categories, one for members of Indiana Rural Youth and one for Farm Bureau women.

The women's department sponsors selection at the district level of the best amateur talent to participate in the State Fair program each year. The department has given, since 1929, from the Gertrude Modlin Memorial Fund (now a part of the Farm Bureau Foundation) a total of $30,875 in scholarships. A few pennies dropped into the collection box at the local Farm Bureau meeting have meant aid to hundreds of young men and women. One scholarship per district is given to qualified young men enrolled in the Purdue Winter Short Course in Agriculture; and one per district to a qualified young woman enrolled in an institution of higher learning.

Women have also distributed health cards to members, so that the health record can be kept on the person at all times against danger from improper care in emergencies. They sponsored the purchasing and presentation of books from the Freedom Bookshelf, a selection of volumes which interpret the role of America in the search for freedom. These books are bought by the local Farm Bureau and presented to local school or public libraries.

The women also promote and give guidance to Pet and Hobby Clubs, for children up to ten years of age—a program unique to Indiana. The clubs meet simultaneously with the adults, but separately, thus encouraging the attendance of young farm couples at the Farm Bureau meeting. The Pet and Hobby leaders teach simple lessons in citizenship, elementary crafts and games.

Cash awards and plaques are given to one rural church in each Farm Bureau district each year for the most outstanding effort to modernize and improve the church's physical facilities and its program. The department also issues suggestions for study and discussion at the local Farm Bureau meeting.

The Indiana Farm Bureau women are a constituent society of the Associated Country Women of the World. The incumbent state women's director, Mrs. Guy E. Gross, Whitley county, has also been president of the Country Women's Council, which is an alliance of all U.S. constituent groups in the ACWW.

Many a friendship has been made over a cup of tea served by Farm Bureau women to their town and city counterparts, the wives of businessmen and professional persons. They have shared their farm experiences on tours set up for town visitors. City children have been brought into farm homes, all for the purpose of establishing better understanding of farm problems, and the farm families in turn learning

about the interests of their guests. Women have been
the instigators in many such events.

Directors of the women's program, as administered
by the women's department since 1926, have been:

    Mrs. Ed Hatch, Allen county (deceased)—1926-
      1928

    Mrs. Harry Modlin, Henry county (deceased)—
      1928-1929

    Mrs. Charles W. Sewell, Benton county
      (deceased)—1929-1935

    Mrs. Benjamin Scott, Hendricks county
      (deceased)—1935-1947

    Mrs. Russell Cushman, Hancock county
      (deceased)—1947-1955

    Mrs. Paul Flinn, Johnson county (deceased)—
      1955-1957

    Mrs. Guy E. Gross, Whitley county—1957-

Farm women are never very far removed from the
economic problems which their husbands face daily.
As early at 1923, a Mrs. Moore of Benton county
appeared before an Indiana Farm Bureau board
meeting to present her views on some of the difficulties then existing in the cream, poultry and egg
marketing stations at Otterbein.

The women's state conference, held each February, often reflects this economic interest. While concessions are made to milady's liking for fashion and
glamor, and for the humanitarian problems of our
society, there will always be found on the program
a speaker or two who deal in the cold, hard facts of
the farming business. Although a few women admit

they slip out to the kitchen at the local meeting, to do the supper dishes while a serious discussion is held, most seem to understand and be eager for any new knowledge that extends their horizons beyond the kitchen walls.

When the Farm Bureau women returned home from their 1933 Conference in Indianapolis, they were met at the door by their husbands with the shocking news that the banks had been closed. The Great Depression had hit a new low. As in any crisis, the farm woman's lot was to test the elasticity of the family dollars. The Depression found them as stout-hearted as their partners.

When asked what today's Farm Bureau woman should consider as her role in the organization, a veteran leader said: "To keep the U's in Farm Bureau; it would mean nothing without them." The you's in the organization are the members, principally as they serve and participate at the local level. Without widespread and continuing participation, doing the little things that make a meeting a success, extending the hand of friendship, helping in community affairs as a representative of agriculture, women would find their organization enfeebled. Feminine enthusiasm and imagination can often save a meeting from being a humdrum affair.

Chapter II
Proliferation of Cooperatives

Producers Marketing Association

Since the marketing of livestock was the source of the most serious complaints among farmers prior to the organization of Farm Bureau it was here the first commercial venture really took hold.

The new Federation encouraged the formation of local shipping associations, although some were operating before it was formed. In the shipping associations, livestock were gathered at a central point either for shipping to a terminal or to be sold to a local buyer at whatever price he might name. There were about one hundred such associations in Indiana in the early twenties.

Before this time, farmers had driven their livestock, often on foot, to the nearest market; sometimes they would take them by wagon or truck. Rail cars, when this form of transportation was called for, were often in short supply. Conditions were much as they are today in underdeveloped countries where beef and sheep are herded many miles on foot to market.

While little benefit to price was noted from the shipping associations' efforts, they did ease the transportation problem. From areas near a terminal, farmers sometimes combined their shipments, shared the transportation costs and sold their animals to the highest bidder at the terminal. But all these efforts had little effect on the market, which dropped as much as $7 a hundredweight within a few days while retail meat prices had risen. Many times the live-stock didn't bring enough to pay shipping costs.

It should be stressed here that if the livestock were sold to a local buyer, it brought one price regardless of grade. Those farmers who took their animals to a terminal market had learned that quality there brought a premium price. The shipping associations served to arouse farmers to the needs for a further step in farmer control of marketing, and for improved quality of livestock.

The associations also surfaced leadership. For example, James Cummins of Jay county, rose through this experience to become fourth district Farm Bureau director, and for many years a director of the Indiana State Fair. He is said to have been the originator of the Farmers' Day parade, now held annually and to which Farm Bureau contributes half the prize money. Cummins' son, W. R., is the present general manager of Producers Marketing Association, Indianapolis, a Farm Bureau affiliate.

William H. Settle, who headed the Wells county shipping association, later became director of the livestock department, then president of Indiana Farm Bureau. Anson S. Thomas and Oscar Swank, who later held prominent roles in the agricultural and organizational development, were leaders in the Montgomery county shipping association.

Conditions at the Indianapolis terminal were so bad that farmers were virtually driven to do some-thing about the problem. The shipping associations of

northeastern Indiana met in Ft. Wayne in 1920 to
study the possibility of forming a statewide marketing
co-operative.

E. J. Trosper of Chicago, the organizing secretary
of the National Federation of Co-operative Livestock
Shippers, was present to report on activity in other
states. Already Michigan and Minnesota had organized, Indiana farmers were told.

At the instance of state Farm Bureau leaders,
P. C. Ohler had been working for a time as a representative of farmers at the Indianapolis stockyards.
While he had done the best he could to guard their
interests, farmers soon realized they would have to
move into the selling operation with an organization
of their own. Settle, who was later to help organize
livestock co-ops in other states, was convinced
Indiana farmers should move in that direction, if
they were to get better prices.

Let us here review some of the conditions that
justifiably irked farmers. Animals were being
weighed on scales that broke at ten pounds, so that
the buyer actually received free of charge all weights
that broke under ten-pound units. A hog that weighed
209 pounds, for example, was bought at 200 pounds.

Animals were not fed and watered properly when
they were unloaded. Many died in trucks or rail cars,
while waiting to be unloaded. They were cuffed and
bruised in handling, then the price was docked because of those bruises. All truck and wagon shipments were sold twice in the yards, once to dealers

who resold them to packers, and the more commission the handlers enjoyed, the less the farmer received.

The new producers' marketing agency, which opened for business May 15, 1922, was at first called the Indianapolis Producers' Commission Agency. D. L. Swanson of Chicago was named manager of the new operation, which proposed to receive livestock on consignment, withhold operating expenses in the form of a commission and return the remainder of the receipts to the farmer. In the first seven months, the new marketing co-op handled $1 million worth of livestock. For the first time, the members' livestock was "In the Hands of a Friend from Beginning to End"—the agency's slogan for many years.

Also during the first year, the scales were adjusted to break at five pounds instead of ten, a practice which continues to this day.

After the Producers' was founded the yards management made a public pronouncement that they were ready to co-operate with farmers. Improvements mere made in rapid order thereafter.

The loyalty of Indiana farmers to their new livestock co-operative is illustrated in a story by Scott Doup, told on himself. In the early days of Farm Bureau, a Columbus newspaper had carried an advertisement from a local packer urging farmers to sell their livestock to a close-at-home market.

"Young and fiery as I was, I talked the officers of the township Farm Bureau into answering the ad with a big display telling the farmer he should ship to an open, competitive market—Indianapolis."

Doup says the Farm Bureau ad even maligned the other firm for calling itself a market. "This is amusing in the light of my later working 12 years for Farmers Marketing Association. (Farm Bureau affiliate) at Columbus to provide the farmer with a near-at-home market. That was followed by sixteen years with the Producers at their near-at-home market," he relates.

It was this kind of unswerving loyalty that assured the success of the co-operative livestock venture.

When the Chicago Livestock Producers' Commission Agency was reorganized in 1926, after having been suspended by the U.S. Department of Agriculture, Swanson was called back to that city to manage it.

Scott Meiks of Shelby county was named to manage the Indianapolis Producers. Meiks had been livestock director for Indiana Farm Bureau and had served four years as state vice-president. He was also a director of the Cleveland Producers and president of the Cincinnati Producers. This wealth of experience was most valuable in getting the new Indianapolis co-operative moving.

Lee Highlen, who had been active in the shipping associations at Liberty Center and Bluffton, was named Indiana Farm Bureau livestock director to succeed Meiks. Oscar Swank was named his assistant, only to move on soon as manager of the Evansville

Livestock Producers' Association, then later to direct the Indiana program of the American Dairy Association for many years.

In the first four years of the Indianapolis Producers' agency, it refunded $125,000 to Indiana farmers. It also stopped existing commission firms, through competition, from raising their charges from $12 to $15 per carload. In that span of years, this act alone meant savings to farmers of $600,00. The firm had also set aside a reserve of $60,000; and, it must be remembered, this was accomplished in a period when economic conditions were anything but favorable to agriculture. These figures constitute an emphatic answer to those who would question the value of farmer-owned co-ops.

Producers' had also brought about increases of 50 to 75 cents per hundredweight on hogs; and $1.50 to $2 on sheep and lambs.

Anson Thomas, who later became Indiana Farm Bureau's tax and legislative director, was first employed as a livestock fieldman. In those days, the Producers' office at the Stockyards was a bit cramped. He recalls having to stoop to get into the place.

James K. Mason of Fayette county is said to have sold the first load of hogs through the Producers' Association, Indianapolis. It is significant to note that the first week's business more than paid the operating costs even at the start.

Changes occurring in transportation were also beginning to affect the livestock picture. The coming of more and more trucks soon outmoded the shipping associations. Montgomery county alone had sold as many as 700 carloads of hogs per year through their shipping association. But change was unavoidable.

Quality came to mean more as the farmer saw the wide range in prices being paid at the terminal. It became a challenge to try for the top market.

But the Producers' got off to a good start and kept pace with change. In recent years, as packers began to move to the country to buy hogs at the farm, so has the Producers' Association. It now has 22 facilities readily accessible to farmers in all parts of the state.

The Producers' Co-operative is guided by a 13-member board of directors, including a director-at-large, who has traditionally been the president of the parent Indiana Farm Bureau organization. Its more than 31,000 patrons are from nearly all parts of the state and east central Illinois. It is a co-operative stock corporation.

Presently this co-op offers breeding and feeder livestock to farmers. Producers' currently sells more than half of all the lambs marketed in Indiana, and they are sold on a graded basis. The co-op provides personnel to aid in a number of pig and calf auctions in southern Indiana each year. They also co-operate with the Indiana Farm Bureau Co-operative Association and local Farm Bureau Co-ops in a feeder pig program, which encourages some 500 farmers to produce about 65,000 feeder pigs annually, these to be sold to other farmers for feeding out for the market. The Indiana Farm Bureau Co-operative Association's feed department sets up the feeding program and the Producers' arranges the contracts and remains in the picture when the market hogs are sold. This combined production and marketing program for high-quality pork in known as the Tend-R-Leen program.

Quality meat-type hogs only are used in this breeding program in order to produce pork more nearly to consumer preference than has been done in the past. Actual retail tests have proved that consumers will pay more for lean pork than for overly fat cuts.

Indiana continues to rank third in the nation in its production of hogs, and the Producers' Marketing Association ranks among the largest hog sales associations in the U.S. This strength and that of the Columbus, Ohio, Producers' were combined in May, 1958, in the formation of Eastern Order Buyers, Inc. EOB is a jointly-owned hog sales agency for the two associations and its benefits have redounded to the farmer's benefit.

From those days when farmers were constantly disgruntled over the manner in which their livestock was handled at the yards, the industry has come a long way. Today, the early morning air at the Indianapolis terminal is rent by the din of thousands of squealing hogs and bawling cattle. Hawk-eyed salesmen move among the pens to encourage a likely bidder. The whole day's business is expedited with order and efficiency.

While the number of patrons has declined from 70,000 to 31,000 today the drop is due to a decline in the number of farmers in the state, a fact reflected in every co-op. It tells the story of agriculture, fewer farmers but greater production per farmer and a greater total.

In 1967, the Producers' Association at Indianapolis marketed 1,041,572 hogs. Total volume of business for that year was $76,166,343.

Country Producers' markets have definitely stimulated local competition and prices. Through the use of certified breeding stock in the feeder pig program, pork quality has made great strides.

By directing their sights toward better service and better prices for livestock farmers, they have developed a program to co-ordinate marketing and improve the quality of pork being produced. Thus, consumption, it is hoped, will be stimulated and even better prices will result.

The growth of the swine industry in this state has been due largely to the joint efforts of hog producers working through Farm Bureau, whose leaders recognized the nature of their problems early in the organization. In a resolution offered in 1919, William Bosson, Marion county farmer, pointed to one of the specific problems: "There is a law on the statute books of Indiana compelling shippers of stock to pay for cleaning cars in which stock has been shipped to market. This is the only state with such a law."

Thanks to Farm Bureau, this and many other inequities have been corrected and the industry now enjoys an economically healthy status. This was accomplished through corrective legislation and the co-operation of Producers' management.

Since all farm prices were low in the early twenties and were making little show of gaining strength, every farmer had his own idea about what kind of co-op would serve his needs. If he grew livestock, he was most interested in the new Producers' agency. If he grew wheat, then he wanted a grain co-op organized; if onions were his specialty, then he wanted help in that field.

On the heels of these demands from varied interests, a rash of exchanges and co-operatives sprang up. At first, it was believed that an exchange would pool the commodity, centralize the selling operation and, by dint of its size, demand better prices for the product. While their premise had been true, they had to learn that the number of co-op patrons and their production volume determined its effectiveness in the market. It was true of many of these early efforts that there were enough farmers outside the pooling effort to offset whatever leverage the co-op had hoped to create. So the exchanges all died in time.

Wool Growers Unite

During World War I, the pooling of wool had been practiced in Putnam and Shelby counties when raw wool was worth about 60 cents per pound. Wool producers began selling to the Ohio Wool and Sheep Growers' Association by contracts drawn up in February, 1921. By this time, farmers had learned that contracts were necessary because of the fact that independent buyers at shearing time would invade an area in an attempt to disrupt the pool.

Actually, pooling had stimulated interest in bidding and grading. Farmers had become aware of what constituted a quality product; and as might be expected, good farmers were happy with the results. Before this, all wool was bought at about the same price, a practice which tended to depress the market. In fact, in one township, farmers took advantage of an offer to trade their wool for blankets and pledged 1,100 pounds in the deal, rather than sell their wool on the open market.

T. I. Ferris, first Steuben county Farm Bureau president, was leader of Indiana wool marketing from 1920 till 1947 and contributed a great deal to stabilize the product at higher prices than had previously been paid. In 1921, Indiana producers pooled 1,200,000 pounds of wool for the Ohio Producer's Association, and at much better prices than were offered locally. This was one-third of the Indiana clip. In 1920 Steuben county farmers alone had shipped 50,000 pounds to the Ohio co-op.

Sponsored by the Indiana Farm Bureau from the first, pooling was done through the wool marketing department of the organization with Ferris directing the operation. Education in grading was conducted at local meetings with interest running high among the women who were interested in getting better wool in their blankets. The price of wool doubled from 1920 to 1926.

In the latter year, the Indiana Wool Growers' Association was incorporated, to operate as an independent unit until 1947 when it was merged with the Indiana Farm Bureau Co-operative Association.

In the meantime handling margins had been reduced. Truck transportation and freight rates made it advisable to pool in Indiana and sell in Indiana. The market became highly competitive. Grading was done at cost by the IFBCA, and then selling was shifted to a national agency, the National Wool Marketing Corporation, which with its twenty-three state members is the largest of its kind in the nation.

County co-ops at the present collect the wool, bring it to the state warehouse in Indianapolis, from whence it is shipped east for marketing to textile mills.

Since shearing time is a very busy time on the farm, the county co-ops initiated a shearing service which has proved a great boon to the wool business.

The very interesting chemical process which con-

verts soil nutrients into plants and plants into animal
life, which through the metabolic process produces
fiber (wool), accounts for an annual farm income
in Indiana of $1,518,000. And in the process,
soldier and civilian alike are made a little more
snug against the biting winds of winter.

Onion Growers Exchange

Next to organize were the onion growers in
northern Indiana; the date, May, 1920. With
the help of Farm Bureau, an exchange was established to be called the Indiana Farm Bureau Onion
Exchange. Charles M. Morgan was employed to
direct oraginzation work. S. D. Dipert of St. Joseph
county was the first president and general manager
of sales. Headquarters were at Warsaw.

Heretofore these onion growers had been selling
to nine markets only. Under the new exchange plan,
a wider area of competition was introduced, and in
one year, they sold 500 carloads of onions to 88
markets in 23 states. The first 300 cars brought a
total of $183,430.

In 1925, the onion pool decided to act as its own
sales agency, and thereupon began its demise since
it was not large enough nor experienced enough to
influence the market.

By this time, farm leaders were beginning to
understand the principles of business in those days
of rugged individualism. On August 6, 1920,
Everett McClure, tenth district Farm Bureau

director, also master of the Indiana Grange, said:

"There are two solutions. One is to get into the rough and tumble game of business and follow out the Sapiro plan, pool our stuff and sign up iron-clad contracts; or we must appeal to the government to regulate big business so that we will be able to market our stuff at a reasonable profit." Aaron Sapiro was a co-operative organizer who had had some success in California.

At that time, it is recorded, the cost of processing and distribution of food was 63 cents of every dollar spent at retail by customers. Today that figure is about 61 cents.

McClure's analysis of the choice open to the Federation was indicative of the fact they had not yet made up their minds on how far to move into marketing. Many were reluctant to go beyond the barnyard gate. They did not see themselves as businessmen—manufacturers of food; so the Onion Association did not last long.

Dairy Marketing

In the early part of this century, every farmer had one or two cows, primarily to supply his family with dairy foods. After the family had drunk what it wanted and had churned the cream into butter, the skim milk was fed to the hogs.

Often the homemaker would trade butter for groceries. Since this was before there was electricity on the farm, there was no satisfactory way to refrigerate milk. Consequently, butter made under these conditions was of poor quality. While some homes had ice boxes, they were not adequate to the need. The cellar often served as a repository for the vessels which contained the milk.

It can readily be seen that the butter that made its way to the grocery was often less than good, often rancid. The grocer sometimes would accept it in order not to offend his farm customer.

When consumers complained of the quality of dairy products found in the grocery store, that dissatisfaction was soon reflected in lower prices. Local dairy co-operatives sprang up in an effort to correct the situation.

On November 11, 1921, articles of incorporation of the Indiana Dairy Marketing Association were ratified at an Indianapolis conference for the purpose of uniting these local co-ops. J. B. Carney, Shelby county, was its first president. C. R. George, Boone county, was secretary-treasurer and director of dairy marketing for the Indiana Federation of Farmers' Associations.

George, a graduate of Ohio State University, had been a member of the Purdue faculty before joining the Federation staff. He immediately set about to encourage the opening of more local cream stations. Some of those already operating bought not only cream but also eggs. Some of the stations were unwisely located. Many farmers considered dairying only as a sideline, so there was not sufficient volume generated.

It proved out that the Indiana Dairy Marketing Association was only a paper organization, set up to guide the activities of the cream stations. Since local farmers had little voice in the stations' operations, they were not much interested in their success and sold to them only if they happened to be near. This lesson is pointed up again and again in the Farm Bureau story. When there is local control, there will be participation and a vigorous program. If that control gets too far away from the farmer, he loses interest.

In the more productive dairy areas in those days, there would be several cream stations within a county. It is recorded that in 1923 six such outlets were doing a monthly volume of $100,000.

In time these stations gave way to larger regional ones as trucks made longer hauls possible. Manufacturing plants began to buy direct at the farm. Milk was converted to cheese, butter, condensed or powdered milk. The exploding population of cities and better understanding of the nutritional value of dairy products began to create a greater demand.

In response to this increased demand, manufacturing and bargaining co-operatives were established on a regional basis. The milk shed, or area within which milk is sold to a central market, has determined the location of these co-ops. At the present time there are farmer-owned dairy co-operatives serving nearly every corner of the state.

The Farm Bureau-sponsored Mid-West Producers Creameries, Inc., founded in 1932, is a supply and merchandising agency with offices now in South Bend. Earl Martin was its first manager, a post now held by E. J. Ryger. Mid-West embraces co-ops in Indiana, Michigan, Iowa, Tennessee, Ohio and Illinois. As early as 1935 Mid-West was selling 30 million pounds of butter per year.

That butter, selling under the name of Valley Lea, is a powerful argument for producing a quality product. The Farmers Marketing Association at Columbus manufactured butter under this label until 1966; and Fred Suhre, for many years manager there, once said that he never had to sell butter. He always had orders telegraphed in advance by eastern buyers who took all its output. People do like good food.

Pure Milk Association of Chicago, another Farm Bureau-sponsored organization, serves the northwest corner of the state and as far east as South Bend. It bottles, manufacturers, and bargains in the Chicago market.

Wayne Co-operative Milk Producers at Ft. Wayne manufactures dairy products there, and operates a milk bottling plant at Cleveland, Ohio. Modern refrigeration can be credited with putting new life blood into the dairy business.

Southeastern Indiana dairy farmers sell to the Cincinnati Milk Sales Association and also to Co-operative Pure Milk Association there. Another dairy co-op was located at Marion, Indiana, but recently merged with Central Indiana Dairymen's Association of Indianapolis. The Vigo County Milk Producers at Terre Haute was also active in the milk bargaining field until it was dissolved in 1967. The Kyana Milk Producers at Louisville and Evansville, and two associations headquartered at Indianapolis continue to serve as milk marketing associations.

The central part of the state is now served by Central Indiana Dairymen's Association, the Miami Valley Milk Producers Association, Wayne Co-operative Milk Producers, Inc. and Pure Milk Association of Chicago. The first is the result of the merger in 1962 of three organizations: Indiana Dairy Producers' Council, Indianapolis Dairymen's Co-operative, and the Howard County Milk Producers.

Today, thirteen co-operative marketing and processing associations serve Hoosier dairymen where dozens were in operation twenty years ago. Authorities point out that population shifts and improvement in milk handling methods account for the smaller number of organizations which can efficiently serve farmers over larger territories.

Indiana Farm Bureau personnel is involved in the activities of the dairy co-ops through educational

and promotional work. The state organization also
supports the American Dairy Association through
its Indiana unit. This is an advertising, merchandising, public relations and research program
financed through a small check-off from the monthly
milk check of the co-operating farmer.

The money is used in timely studies, promotional
demonstrations before high school classes and public gatherings, and for national advertising. The
Association's educational program in recent years
has been directed at teen-agers in the belief that
eating habits formed early will become fixed. More
than twenty-four research projects in experiment
stations across the country were in progress in 1967.
ADA is supported by dairy farmers in the 50 states.
ADA in Indiana is headed by Byron A. Field, who
had eighteen years of dairy marketing experience in
the Evansville area.

The walnut growers of the state tried their hand
early at co-operative marketing, but only for a brief
period. In November, 1921, the Indiana Walnut
Growers' Association was formed, with an assessment of $2.50 per $100 worth of nuts sold. The
group was small and the market limited and the
young co-op died a-borning.

The Drama of Grain

From the beginning of history, the sowing of grain
has been a primary act. It has meant life and
promise. Grains which went into breadstuff existed

at least 2,000 years ago. An imbedded grain has been found in a brick taken from one of the Egyptian pyramids supposedly built in 395 B.C. Excavations of the ancient city of Pompeii in Italy revealed a woman squatting in front of her oven, loaf of bread in hand, fixed in that position by molten lava which buried the city in 79 A.D.

Yes, grain has played a fascinating part in the drama of mankind. Hungry millions around the earth each year await its harvest. In Isaiah 38:6 we are reminded that "all flesh is grass." Whether grasses produce grain for bread or for meat, they are the very substance of life.

Producing and trading in this commodity have always attracted man. In the formative years of this nation, when millions of acres begged to be cleared and planted, there was great opportunity in corn and wheat.

As our population moved westward, and machines were developed to handle the harvest, the grain business soon became complex and vast. The Board of Trade at Chicago became, and still is, the center of grain marketing for the nation.

Since millions of dollars are involved in the Board's transactions, suspicion grew it was exploiting the farmer. Feeding this suspicion in the decade before the organization of Farm Bureau was a fictionalized book, The Pit, by Frank Norris who told this story of alleged exploitation convincingly. This aroused misgivings among farmers about the whole machinery of marketing and distribution, the vast structure which serves the agricultural economy.

In the heat of the national scandal which emerged from the book, Judge L. Gough, president of the Texas Wheat Growers' Association, challenged to debate James A. Patton, called "a Board of Trade operator" on statements made by Patton in a series of articles in the Saturday Evening Post on The Wheat Pit.

The American Farm Bureau Federation, early in its program, named committees to investigate. These men journeyed to the west coast to study co-operative marketing (already advanced in that area) as a possible bulwark against exploitation. Wool, dairy, livestock, and vegetable producers also began to meet at the national level to study their problems. Farmers were moving. Sometimes their actions were misdirected, but they came out fighting.

In the twenties, the whole nation was in a boisterous and aggressive mood. The population and the market were growing. The nation was well served by a network of railroads.

Naturally some grain handlers at the thick of the fray were in business to make all the profit they could. The lure of financial gain has always been intoxicating to the imagination.

The producer and small grain handler, whose positions were not equally favorable, suffered for their lack of market strength. Organized farmers and the federal government began to try to check the threat at about the same time. In Indiana, elevator owners organized the Indiana Grain Dealers' Association in 1920.

Soon afterward, this group joined with the Indiana Federation of Farmers' Associations and the Indiana Grange to establish the Federated Marketing Service. This was a purchasing co-op which lasted only about two years—its failure blamed on lack of coordination of effort and a central management strong enough to make it function.

On the national level, the U.S. Grain Growers' Association was formed in an attempt to stabilize and expedite the marketing of grain. This was in December, 1923. States had been trying to contract farmers to sell their wheat through a pool. The farmer was to be paid part of his money when he delivered the grain, and the rest when the national pool disposed of it. The pooling agency had no facilities of its own, but had to depend on local elevators' cooperation for storage and shipping.

The Indiana pool was organized under the Robert W. Bingham Act of Kentucky for lack of an Indiana law which fitted the situation. Bingham, a newspaper publisher, had become an ardent champion of the farmer. The first drive for members of the pool resulted in 9,000 before harvest time. It was doubled in 1925. James W. Gwaltney of Poseyville was president. The first year of its operation, the pool handled 1,300,000 bushels at prices that ran ten cents about the "outside" market. Then the pool began to have difficulty.

The Indiana Federation of Farmers' Association had advanced $20,000 to the U.S. Grain Growers' Association during its organization period. J. Edgar Scholl of Fayette county recalls his part in the grain venture with embarrassment and apologies; but many Indiana farmers were sincerely searching for a better way to improve their markets. Scholl was only one of many who were learning, with some disillusionment, about the ways of business.

The national agency had proposed to control terminal facilities, warehouses, exporting, and farmer co-operatives. This was a big order. Weaknesses began to be revealed in the whole pooling operation.

Local elevator managers began telling farmers they could get them more money outside the pool. This was at a time when farmers were extremely short of cash. They liked the idea of getting all their money at harvest time. They also disliked the idea of compulsory pooling. It is recorded, that during this period of depressed grain prices, 40 per cent of Indiana wheat was sold within 30 days after harvest. This dumping did the market little good.

An Evansvile milling company was accused of persuading farmers to jump their contracts in that part of the state. Regular grain trade operators began to capitalize on the chinks in the armour.

In 1926, a new attempt was made by grain producers to effect a larger bargaining group which
would be controlled by farmers. Named the Central
Growers' Association, it included Indiana, Ohio,
and Illinois, with Indiana's president, William H.
Settle as manager. The Indiana member of the
group was known as the Indiana Grain Growers'
Association with its offices in the Indiana Farm
Bureau headquarters in Indianapolis. In 1926, the
year the three states united, the Indiana pool handled four million bushels of wheat on a declining
market.

The contract in those days was regarded as the
only tool that could make their co-operative effort
succeed. However, though they were legally bind-
ing, some farmers regarded contracts lightly.

A tabloid edition of The HOOSIER FARMER
was distributed at the 1925 convention which
reported "the trial and conviction" of Frank Arn, a
farmer who had violated his contract. Arn was
shown behind bars. While all this was done in fun,
it probably intended to restore respect for the
legality of the contract.

In October, 1923, the National Wheat Growers'
advisory committee was named to serve as watchdog in the trade. Wheat prices in those days were
dictated by the Liverpool, England, market. Our
price for grain was the price in Liverpool minus
freight charges. Midwest farmers soon saw that to

reduce those freight charges, they needed a deep waterway to the Atlantic Ocean.

The 1923 Seventy-Third Indiana General Assembly, which came to be known as the "farmers' Legislature" appropriated $12,000 for a study of the possibility of getting a St. Lawrence seaway— an effort that later extended into a demand for a deep water port on Lake Michigan on Indiana's northern shoreline. In recent years, the deep channel has been completed, and an Indiana port is under construction.

In the co-operative efforts in the grain business, farmers learned an important lesson—that it is best to start at the local level and then— very important —to merge local units into a strong bargaining and service organization. Those who participated in the pioneering ventures that failed should feel no shame. The ground had to be "plowed." The lesson was learned in the plowing.

After several years of trying to operate the grain business and at the same time direct the course of the Farm Bureau out of the office of the Farm Bureau president, all the time having to turn to the newly formed Indiana Farm Bureau Co-operative Association for temporary financial assistance, Indiana Farm Bureau officers decided to organize the grain business into a co-operative. It was called the Indiana Grain Co-operative. This was in 1938 and M. D. Guild, Pulaski county, who became one of the best grain men in the nation, was named the first manager.

Another development should be injected into this story. In 1919 there were about 600 local co-operative elevators in the state, according to an estimate made by I. H. Hull in his book, Built of Men. Mergers occurred rapidly, until today there are about one-third that many. The county Farm Bureau co-ops now own and operate about 225 local elevators. This trend to fewer and fewer outlets was a foregone conclusion. Factors of transportation and efficiency made the mergers advisable.

The state grain co-operative as yet had no storage facilities, one of the first essentials to a strong bargaining position in grain. With the assistance of Indiana Farm Bureau Co-operative Association leaders, an Indianapolis elevator was purchased.

Guild had been district manager of the National Grain Co-operative, which was an effort to stabilize the market and stop speculation, a venture that failed because of government domination, according to M. J. Briggs. Lack of financial resources and poor management caused its downfall. The more than two million dollars left from that enterprise was turned over to the Bank for Co-operatives in 1933.

The Indiana Grain Co-operative was merged with the Indiana Farm Bureau Co-operative Association in 1950, a move deemed advisable because of the rapid growth of the grain business and the role of the IFBCA in maintaining a flow of capital adequate for this growth. It is now known as the grain division of the IFBCA, which today has storage space for 22 million bushels in warehouses in Indianapolis, Princeton, Louisville, Kentucky, Chicago, Illinois, Baltimore, Maryland and country elevators located throughout Indiana. It also has storage for shipping from the deep water port at Toledo, Ohio.

All grain warehoused by the IFBCA is hedged by selling the equivalent amount on the futures market. Local co-op elevator managers are trained periodically in the handling and proper drying of grain, and in blending grades to get a better market price for the farmer.

In the Indianapolis office of the co-op grain division, nine telephone lines are kept busy from 8 until 9:30 a.m. each day transacting the business indigenous to the grain industry. The farmer should frequently remind himself that in every transaction, he is there; his interests are being protected.

During harvest season, the volume handled in such transactions runs from one to one and one-half million bushels daily. Annual business involves some 60 million bushels. Cash sales are handled through the Indianapolis office direct with the buyers and the grain futures market of the Chicago Board of Trade is utilized in carrying out the hedging operations.

The end result of all this endeavor can be measured in one statement: In spite of the tremendous increase in handling costs, *the handling margin for*

*grain is now about one-third what it was when
farmers started to do something to improve grain
marketing*

During the early twenties, all farm prices were
undergoing a decline. The purchasing power of the
dollar stood at 69. An increase in freight rates,
together with tightened credit regulations, served to
further complicate the farm problem.

The man who had directed the course of the new
farm organization during the early trial and error
period was John G. Brown of Monon, first president
of the Federation.

John G. Brown of White county was a common
man but not an ordinary one. His most outstanding
qualities which came in good stead during the
Federation's first four years were caution and pru-
dence. He was also basically honest, a characteristic
quickly sensed by the people.

Mr. Brown was the product largely of his own
efforts. He had been a day laborer working by the
month, a tenant farmer, then owner of a small farm.
Finally he acquired and operated a considerable
acreage.

More than six feet tall, awkward and gangling, he
never failed to inspire the members' confidence. The
fluctuating fortunes of the organization's commercial
enterprises were not taken as casting any doubt on
their leader's reliability. As a contemporary said:
"He was a man of high morals and good character."

The first president delineated his basic regard for

agriculture in a talk in Union County (where his father was born) when he said:

"In order to swing the trend of our young people back to the farm, we must dignify farming; we must equalize industrial labor hours with farm labor hours; and we must improve country living conditions."

Later in the same talk he pointed to some of the pitfalls ahead of the organization:

"One of the greatest dangers of a large, powerful organization is an abuse of its power. This must never happen. We stand for a square deal for all . . . We intend to see farmers' interests are protected."

President Brown's slow and deliberate approach to a problem won for him and the organization the confidence of the business community. His cob pipe and innate caution were always in evidence.

On the occasion of his second election in 1920 (term of office was one year at the time) he spelled out the farm problem in realistic terms:

"As producers (we) have met organized buying with unorganized selling; as consumers we have met organized selling with unorganized buying." This was the major problem in 1920 and in some commodities it is the major problem of the sixties, although with less severity.

Though cautious by nature, Brown would resort to quick action when it was called for. A railroad strike during his term of office threatened to hamper the normal flow of farm products to market — a debacle the farmer could ill afford. This telegram was sent to President Woodrow Wilson: "If the railroad strike continues, we seriously contemplate advising all members to hold their farm products until the strike ends."

While this action never took place, the threat did indicate that a capacity for punitive action was there in this pioneer leader.

During the July, 1919, meeting held in Indianapolis, farmers congregated there were to learn their president was in Washington, in company with some state officials, to plead with the U.S. Department of Agriculture to lift a quarantine on wheat. Government action had been taken because of the presence in Indiana of an Australian disease called Take-All.

A quick check found that it existed in only a few counties in the northwestern part of the state. The Department agreed that if only those counties affected could be quarantined, the measure affecting the entire state would be lifted. This action on the part of President Brown saved Indiana wheat farmers thousands of dollars that year.

Brown and Dean J. H. Skinner of the Purdue School of Agriculture were good friends. In fact, they owned a farm jointly in later years. To some this relationship was desirable; to others, it appeared to aggravate an ever present problem—that of the need for Farm Bureau to build an independent policy-making organization.

In 1921, as president, Brown played a prominent role in organizing the National Livestock Producers'

Association, of which he was named its first president. He was also on the executive committee of the American Farm Bureau Federation, and a member of the board of directors of the Ohio Sheep and Wool Growers' Association.

When Brown stepped down from the office of Federation president, it was by choice. He wanted to return to his farm. But to him goes the credit of having kept alive during those difficult and hazardous years an organization later to become a potent force in Indiana agriculture and in local and state government.

Frequent Moves

In the meantime state headquarters of the Federation had been moved from Room 369 in the English Hotel to the Lemcke Building, 147 East Market Street, Indianapolis,—a chore which required only two suitcases and the energies of Lewis Taylor, then general secretary. At first two rooms were rented. Later the whole floor was needed to accommodate the growing organization and the new Mutual Insurance Company. For a brief time, FB was housed on North Senate, then in the Old Trails Building, 309 West Washington Street, before joining with the state co-op and the insurance companies in 1947 to buy a building at 47 South Pennsylvania for all three organizations.

Growth of the insurance companies necessitated a move, this time across the street on Pennsylvania to the Century Building. When the U.S. Government exercised eminent domain and took over that structure, the two organizations moved again. The joint building ownership was dissolved; the IFBCA bought out the interests of the other organizations and remains at 47 South Pennsylvania today. The parent company is now housed in a building at 130 East Washington Street owned by the insurance companies.

This picture is given in one dose, so to speak, to demonstrate the growing size and affluence of the organizations serving Indiana farmers. From one small room and furnishings that filled only two suitcases, the companies have grown to fulfill their promise of continued service through the Farm Bureau organizations, now occupying many buildings.

Canning Crops Exchange

The move toward more co-operatives continued in the country. In the early twenties when most of these trial balloons were launched, farmers seldom specialized as many do today. A farmer would have some hogs, a few milk cows, and a flock of chickens. He would probably raise a patch of tomatoes or sweet corn or cucumbers. He might try his hand at a spring income from strawberries. Efficiency had not yet been married to specialization.

Because of this situation and others, there was wide interest in the co-operative movement as the answer to his problems.

To improve prices and marketing conditions for growers of tomatoes, one of the more popular vegetables produced, an organization to function like a pool was founded January 15, 1924, with IFB President Settle as chairman.

While the name of this co-op was Indiana Canning Crops Exchange, it dealt primarily with tomatoes as the first commodity upon which to focus efforts. Local groups were to serve as purchasers, and they in turn would become federated with the state exchange. Twenty-two district groups were formed in the first month. H. R. Atcheson, Scott county, was the first president.

The picture brightened immediately. The farmers involved were sure they had found the answer. In Daviess county, tomatoes rose from $10 to $12 per ton the first year; through the state association it rose to $13.50. At Petersburg, they sold through the local pool for $14. While the new co-op could not take full credit, that year's crop brought $400,000 more than had the previous year's.

In February, 1925, 30 canners signed contracts to buy tomatoes through the co-op at $14 per ton, or $4 more than they had paid two years before. Twenty of these canners lived up to their contracts.

The attractive price drew many other farmers into the business of growing tomatoes; then canners turned outside the co-op to buy at a lower figure.

This left the co-op with tomatoes to dispose of. On an experimental basis, these co-op leaders built

18 canning plants located in areas where need was indicated. They were located at Matthews, Upland, Wrights, Fowlerton, two at Fairmount—all in Grant county; Rushville, Paragon, two at Newberry in Greene county; at Jordan and Plainville in Daviess county; at Rogers and two at Petersburg in Pike county; Jasper, Oaktown in Knox county; and at Carlisle in Sullivan county.

John W. Ritter of Daviess county, who had been made general manager and organization director for the vegetable co-op, in a report to the 1925 state convention, stated that the canning factories had been most successful in areas remote frome large towns and railroads, where farmers themselves supplied the labor for processing.

Increased production and the loss of buyers spelled the end of this co-op. Farmers found they had hundreds of tons of tomatoes for which there was no market. They turned to canning in five-gallon cans in order to save on operating expenses. This gave rise to their being called "horse tank canners."

Here again the old refrain applied: The co-op did not represent enough volume to exert sufficient influence on the market. Secondly, farmers took no account of the supply factor, and raised more tomatoes than canners could have been justly expected to buy. And third, once they decided to go into the canning business, they found they had overlooked the necessity of a plan to sell their products in canned form.

They probably asked themselves in 1925 as farmers do today: Just how far should we go into the processing and distribution of our products?

❖❖

Chapter III
Services Grow

❖❖

When the Federated Marketing Service disbanded, upon the withdrawal of the Grange and the Grain Dealers' Association, the service was placed in a purchasing department in the Indiana Farm Bureau with Louis Shuttleworth as its first director. It took about one year for FB leaders to see that a better buying and selling program was needed than the purchasing department had provided; besides it found itself with a sizeable deficit.

In 1926 it was reorganized, later to be known as the Indiana Farm Bureau Cooperative Association, with I. H. Hull as general manager for the first twenty years. Then he was president until his retirement in 1950.

Hull, a Northwestern University graduate, who had been president of the LaPorte County Farm Bureau, had cut his organization eye teeth in an Illinois county Farm Bureau before moving to Indiana in 1913. The progressive attitude of LaPorte farmers may be traced to Hull's leadership. That county was the first in the state to have an agricultural agent, called at that time an adviser. He was L. B. Clore sent there on an experimental basis and paid by persons and organizations having agricultural interests. Hull was one of the first to do tractor farming. LaPorte was the first county in the nation to be declared free of bovine tuberculosis, an achievement of which Hull is very proud. Johnson county achieved this feat early in FB history.

Within the first two years of the IFBCA's existence, it was doing more than $2 million in annual business. Today it is the largest farmer-owned co-operative in the nation, doing business within a state.

To Hull fell the task of trying and proving the methods of operation that went into the building of this successful business. He is, by reason of this contribution, known as Mr. Co-op. His ardent zeal carried over into the campaign to establish the Rural Electric Membership Co-operatives. His conviction that co-operatives are necessary to agriculture became an impelling evangelism to spread that philosophy over the state.

Hull stated the purpose of the newly organized co-op as "not for profit but for service to the farmer, —with retention of 25 percent of the savings as reserves."

All sales were at first made for cash. In the 20 years during which Hull was manager, many services were developed which were not included in the original dream back in 1919. At first it merely channeled orders for equipment in carload lots direct to the community wanting it. Next it went into the wholesale business to supply county co-op needs.

The new supply co-op learned early in its existence that to become a permanent boon to the farmer, it must become deeply involved in all facets of the supply and purchasing needs of its patrons. While many small town businessmen resented this invasion of their territory, they came to accept the farmer-owned co-op as just another competitor. Mrs. Edna Shankland, Starke county leader, says co-ops and other businesses serve to keep each other in line.

In keeping with this plan for expansion, the IFBCA has become also a manufacturer of plant food, owner of oil wells and refiner of petroleum products. To control costs further still, it has invested in sources of supply for ingredients that go into fertilizers

It must be remembered that the distribution outlets did not develop overnight. A wholesaler must have outlets. At first the counties handled supplies on a commission basis and no state reserves were set up. Later Co-op officials decided that to make their prices competitive and then pass back the earnings as patronage refunds would be the wiser course.

These refunds are paid to the county co-ops, some in cash and some in stock certificates. In 1966, the 84 county outlets returned to farmers in cash a total of $2,036,813. This included cash refunds, common stock redeemed, and dividends on both common and preferred stock. The total cash returned during the ten-year period prior to and including '66 was $19,607,845. It must be realized that this was money, which before the organization of the IFBCA, never reached farmers' pockets.

County co-ops are governed by local boards of directors. Patronage refunds may be passed on to the farmer or held for improvement or expansion purposes, except for that percentage which federal law specifies must go to the farmer in cash.

The going has not been easy for the co-operative supply business. It has been difficult to get farmers weaned away from brands of equipment and supplies they were accustomed to using. In the machinery business, co-ops themselves have been to blame when they were reluctant or unprepared to service the equipment they sold. In some counties, agency contracts were signed by the local co-op directly with another manufacturer.

Farmers' demand for a better farm tractor led Indiana Co-op leaders to develop one with two innovations—rubber tires and a high compression motor. After ninety-two county demonstrations in Indiana, and despite sabotage of a gas line by a competitor, the tractor made its debut in 1935.

The IFBCA was joined in this venture by wholesale co-operatives from four other states. The contract for manufacture was written with an established company. By 1940 this joint venture was dissolved and the Indiana Co-op built its own assembly plant at Shelbyville, Indiana. It made contracts for distribution throughout the country and seemed to be on its way. But the need for greater quantities of steel in the conduct of the Second World War made it necessary to allocate it for domestic use. Since the Co-op had no history of manufacture, it had no base for allocation.

The Shelbyville plant was eventually closed and the operation moved to Ohio. But due to many factors—the preference of farmers for other lines of equipment for which they had a prejudiced attachment, the failure of the local co-ops to service properly the machinery they sold—the IFBCA decided in 1962 to get out of the heavy machinery business altogether.

There are three distinct areas in which the co-op serves farmers today—offering farm supplies, marketing farm products, and conducting research. The last named has become one of the most vital in view of rapidly changing agricultural science.

First efforts in research in the IFBCA were made a number of years ago when Thad Macy, head of the poultry and hatchery department, successfully isolated pullorum disease which is transmitted in the egg. Despite some scoffing from the professionals, Macy, through control of flocks on a farm near Spencer, proved his control method for the sickness that was at the time decimating Indiana poultry flocks. This step alone launched the broiler program in the state on a profitable basis.

There has always been an excellent working relationship between the IFB and the Purdue Agricultural Experiment Station. Farm Bureau and the state FB Co-op serve most of the farmers in the state; so whatever need is expressed, by way of research, often becomes a command performance at the Station.

In addition to this source of help, the Co-op has
joined with a number of other state farmer-owned
co-ops over the nation in a number of research areas.
This group is conducting feed tests with broilers at
Talmo, Georgia; turkeys at Anoka, Minnesota; a lay-
ing flock at Garner, North Carolina; with swine and
beef at Lexington, Illinois; dairy cattle at Fabius,
New York; and twin dairy calves at Sunnyside,
Washington.

The IFBCA has its own poultry research farm
near Lafayette, Indiana, where as many as 25,000
birds at one time are involved in genetic studies.
Whatever the findings of all this scientific delving,
they become a guide to the co-op program of service
to farmers.

The manufacture of improved, open-formula
feeds occurs at the Farm Bureau Milling Company,
Hammond, purchased in 1943; at the new South-
west Indiana Feed Mill at Loogootee; and at a new
feed mill at Princeton, Indiana.

Under the initiative of Harry Truax, now retired,
who headed the feed department for IFBCA many
years, local co-ops were encouraged to install their
own mixing equipment so that the farmer could
add his own grain to formula mixes. This move
proved popular with farmers.

As today's man on the land becomes less and less
self-sufficient because of the industrial and technological revolution, he finds himself more dependent on his co-operative for economic and scientific

protection. This was acutely true in his requirements for oil and gasoline. Where he once grew fuel for animal horsepower, he now found himself having to buy fuel for motorized horsepower.

While the embryonic co-op was still the purchasing department of the Indiana Farm Bureau, a flier was taken in oil through contracts with two established oil companies who agreed to supply it and pay a commission of five cents per gallon. The offer was attractive for two reasons: (1) the state treasury was in need of money; (2) leaders saw in it a chance to get more members, since a farmer would be required to have a membership before he was paid the patron's share of the commission. In their eagerness for these two benefits, they overlooked the factor of quality which they had supposed they would be getting.

This was before there were established standards for such products. Farmers later learned that the oil and gas they were using in their tractors were damaging them. Contracts were canceled, but farmers had acquired the habit of looking to their co-op for these products.

In 1929 the IFBCA set up its own testing and blending facility at Indianapolis, the first real industrial venture of the organization. In nine months, this new development had earned enough to pay for the installation, had met competitive prices and had given farmers quality oil.

Since that time a refinery has been built at Mount Vernon, Indiana, wells drilled in southern Indiana and Illinois, and a pipeline laid to carry both oil and gasoline into the northern part of the state. The future of this endeavor depends on a continuing supply of crude oil and upon trained, efficient men to direct the operation.

The IFBCA also owns a seed plant at Crawfordsville, bought in 1945, to buy and process seeds of quality. More than 125 carloads of legume and grass seeds are distributed each year. A plant breeding program got under way in 1962 with the purchase of a farm of 72 acres near Battle Ground, Indiana. Research there is conducted by Forage Research Co-operative, a joint effort of several regional co-ops.

Through its investment in Central Farmers' Fertilizer Company of Chicago, IFBCA is associated with nitrogen production in Louisiana, phosphate production in Florida, and potash production in New Mexico and Canada. It also has an investment in Central Nitrogen, Inc., at Terre Haute, a manufacturer of nitrogen plant food.

Indiana farmers market more than 60 million bushels of grain and 1,700,000 pounds of wool each year through the state Co-op. The farmer-businessman of Indiana, through this sprawling, progressive Co-op has acquired an interest in property worth $88,216,000 at the state and local levels. Total sales of the state organization in 1966 were

$190 million. That figure in 1930 was only $4 million.

Good management and full co-operation between the IFB and the IFBCA were necessary to this amazing growth. And let's not forget that free enterprise was responsible. In 1936, during this period of great co-operative expansion in Indiana and the United States as a whole, 73 major con- sumers' co-ops in Germany were dissolved and 72 million marks of savings deposits confiscated in the Nazi program of nationalization—a striking contrast.

Many emerging, underdeveloped nations today are establishing co-operatives as a buffer between the very rich and very poor, and to give the common man his first taste of pride of ownership. Some economists have recommended co-ops as the best safeguard against communism in such areas.

Pure Serum Company

In 1931 the Indiana Farm Bureau bought the majority of the stock in the Swine Breeders' Pure Serum Company at Thorntown, which decided to quit business because of its lack of local distribution points. But hog cholera was still the big threat to every hog producer. IFB President William H. Settle, himself a hog producer, was particularly interested in getting good serum to farmers.

The company became known as the Farm Bureau Serum Corporation, with the change of ownership, and M. S. Barker of Boone county was its manager.

Other manufacturers had begun to make better quality serum available, and veterinarians were turning to them also for other drugs. Farm Bureau had encouraged farmers to administer the serum to their own hogs, and this lost some of the good will of the veterinarians.

After five years of trying to ride the tide, Farm Bureau turned over its interests in the corporation to the Indiana Farm Bureau Co-operative Association. In 1948, the merger was completed when the Co-op bought at par value all stock and certificates of indebtedness.

At that time, an agreement was reached with the veterinarians under which the serum would be sold to them exclusively. County co-ops installed refrigerated storage equipment to take care of the demand, where it existed. But some veterinarians refused to participate in the agreement.

About this time, the Indiana Farm Bureau started its campaign to establish a School of Veterinary Medicine at Purdue—an effort which some "vets" resented because they felt it would train more competition. Although some veterinarians agreed to the need for the School, resentment cut into the serum business still further; and the Co-op sold its interests to a group of "vets" who have added other drugs needed in farm practice.

This whole panorama of activity over the past 45 years has been an epic of men trying desperately to improve their own economic and social conditions. From beginning to end, it is a story of co-operation among Indiana farmers. This new "gospel" was spread in the early days by such men as Russell Van Hook, Jasper county, who in impeccable English leveled his persuasion at many audiences; Dr. W. D. Shelby, Clark county, who had owned and operated a hospital in China for many years, and now, residing on an Indiana farm, turned his missionary zeal toward the cause of the co-operative. There was C. S. Masterson, ex-clergyman and farmer from Hancock county; and of course, I. H. Hull, a most ardent devotee and one of the best informed on the co-operative movement in the nation.

Z. M. Smith of the Purdue Extension Service, who was also Indiana's first state 4-H club leader and first state director of vocational education, together with FB leaders, set up adult classes from 1926-28 to give instruction on co-op principles. Ten lessons were given through the winter months with Lewis Taylor, IFB vice-president, and P. C. Engle of Pulaski county, the instructors. Others were added later. The Federal government bore five-sixths of the cost, and IFB paid the remainder.

Co-op education has continued to be a part of the program. The IFBCA conducts special classes, meetings or trips for farm youth, co-op managers, and others. Discussion of co-op operations has its periodic place in the local FB meeting.

Through these commercial ventures and a broader understanding of the vital role of the co-op in the farm operation, the Indiana farmer today is following his products to ever more remote points of distribution. Wool, grain, poultry and livestock now seek out the best markets, domestic and foreign. Rapid transportation has helped make this possible.

The American Farm Bureau Federation maintains an office in Chicago, where it makes contacts with buyers of agricultural products. In 1958, 22 farmer-owned regional grain co-operatives, including the IFBCA, established the Producers' Export Company in New York City to expedite grain exports. Eastern Order Buyers, Inc., a subsidiary of the Producers Marketing Association, moves livestock into eastern markets and foreign trade.

Many individual farmers are grading their products, packaging them under a brand name, or processing them before they leave the farm. This is more especially true of fruit, vegetable, and poultry farmers. They are reading the handwriting on the wall.

National and State Recognition

None can say whether fate plays a hand in putting the right man in the right place at the right time, or whether that man grows to fit the opportunity and the responsibility. One thing is certain. William H. Settle, Wells county breeder of Chester White hogs and dynamic leader, was just what the doctor ordered for the Indiana Farm Bureau in 1923. For 12 years, he applied his energies to making a place for organized agriculture on the state and national scene.

Second IFB president, he was the oldest of nine children. His formal education did not go beyond the fifth grade, although he attended school irregularly after that. His father had lost his health in the Civil War, and much of the family responsibility fell upon the shoulders of young Bill.

As a young man he worked for a time in the oil fields, then ran a livery stable in Montpelier for several years. Later he moved to an 80-acre farm near Phenix, in south Wells county, where he lived until he moved to Indianapolis as the newly elected president of the Indiana Farm Bureau.

He had been active in the local livestock shipping association and was called to Buffalo, N. Y., St. Louis, Mo., and St. Paul, Minn., to help set up producers commission firms in those markets.

Though not an astute businessman, Settle was a natural leader of men, fearless in time of trouble, and unusually independent. He spent a great deal of time in the nation's capital in a continuous effort to enlist support for needed farm legislation. In 1932, at the depth of the Great Depression, the Indiana leader worked untiringly for Congressional support of an equalization fee and debenture plan he had helped to devise. From his many trips to Washington, he was said to have known more Congressmen than any other lay citizen; but Farm Bureau member contacts back home suffered.

The protocol and pomposity of the nation's capital did not faze him. It is even told that he once canceled an appointment with the President of the United States because he considered other business more important. A Washington correspondent at the time said of Settle: "He wears his own spats but no one's collar."

L. L. Needler, former director and long active in both IFB and the state Co-op, got a chuckle from an incident that occurred by Settle's doing. It was when the Indiana president, the American Farm Bureau president, Ed O'Neal, and others were promoting the McNary-Haugen bill in Congress. Settle had heard that Congressman Magnus Johnson, an out-spoken advocate of the bill, had a speaking date at Winona, Indiana, on a rapidly approaching day. He sent word to Perry Crane, IFB secretary, to request that all employees and members of the board of directors load their cars with farmers and come to Winona to hear the notable gentleman.

Needler says: "I lost my way, but we arrived just in time to see Bill come swaggering down the street. He had just debarked from the Chicago-bound Pennsylvania train. I mean no disrespect of Bill Settle. He was a dynamic leader and came to Farm Bureau when it most needed one of his type.

"On this particular day, he was riding high. He came down the street in long strides exuding confidence with every step. He glad-handed us at the door (of the meeting place) and then strode over to the hotel clerk's desk and asked if there was a message for Bill Settle. He was a country boy, learning fast the ways of modern business.

"There was, indeed, a telegram. It read: 'Congressman Johnson will speak in Winona, *Minnesota,* today."

While president, Settle headed the U.S. Grain Growers co-operative and was a member of the Indiana State Fair board of directors for a number of years.

When farmers in southern Indiana started jumping their wheat pool contracts, Settle, accompanied by Oscar Swank, went to a meeting called in Princeton one night to try to pull into line some 100 irate farmers. Their discontent had been fomented by an Evansville milling company which needed their wheat and didn't propose to be stopped by a pool contract. Swank recalls that Settle walked into their midst and did verbal battle with them. Words flew. Some law suits ensued to enforce the terms of the contracts. In time, the grain business became Settle's pride and joy.

One gets the impression in reading of his activities that he was everywhere at once. He undertook a great many responsibilities. However, when offered a post on the Federal Farm Board, an eight-man directive group in the late twenties, Settle declined, saying he could render more service to the farmer through his co-operative. He was actually president of the IFBCA from its founding until 1934, when he resigned to be succeeded by James K. Mason, Fayette county.

Settle and Secretary Crane campaigned through several southern states in behalf of the Dickson bill, another equalization measure. Though the bill was defeated, Settle's efforts had boosted Indiana Farm Bureau's prestige. During that period, it is reported that the Indiana farm leader made speeches in all but two of the first 48 states.

Because of a growing demand from the farmers that property taxes be reduced, Settle and his first vice-president, Lewis Taylor, who was also the tax and legislative director, drew up a plan in response to this farm unrest. They presented the plan to Governor Harry G. Leslie and asked him to call a special session of the legislature to consider it.

Allegedly, the demand for property tax relief had started in Steuben county, where a petition with 3,700 names had originated. By the time their case was presented to the General Assembly, the petition contained 45,000 names. Settle and Taylor were named to a committee by the Governor to go over the plan before the special session. Action was taken by the legislators which set a $1.50 per hundred tax levy limit on real property—a move which effected an annual savings of $30 million. Also in that session, the state budget was reduced by $9 million.

Settle's activities on the national scene brought Indiana agriculture into the limelight—a recognition which it still enjoys both for its leadership and its farm production. A measure of Farm Bureau's and Settle's influence on the Hoosier Congressional delegation is their vote on the McNary-Haugen bill. Only one voted against it the first time. Two years later, when it was re-introduced, Indiana voted solidly for it, only to have it vetoed by President Calvin Coolidge.

Settle also initiated in Indiana the idea that Farm Bureau should make recommendations to the political platform committees. The first such effort was anything but successful, but it later developed as regular procedure during every campaign year, both in the state and the nation. Now the recommendations, based on organization policies, are made by Indiana Farm Bureau to the state Democratic and Republican platform committees, and by the American Farm Bureau to the two national party committees.

After Settle was Indiana Farm Bureau president, he bought a farm of 160 acres near Petroleum, Indiana, where he and Mrs. Settle resided until her death. He then moved to Montpelier to remain until his death in 1953.

Early in Settle's tenure, he made a move which, while it was sound and approved by the board of directors, later led to his ouster. (He had signed a ten-year contract whereby Indiana Farm Bureau would act as agent for the State Farm Mutual Insurance Company of Bloomington, Illinois.) State Farm was a small company in need of a market.

Through contractual arrangement with the Indiana Farm Bureau, Inc., they were given access to the total farm market in Indiana. This provided Indiana farmers with the insurance they needed. Farmers at that time were grossly under-insured and because of this were frequent financial victims of weather and accident. Automobiles and trucks on the farm were becoming commonplace, and rates in existing companies were very high and coverage inadequate. Indiana Farm Bureau had very limited resources at the time, so the thought of starting its own company did not seem feasible.

Just before the contract was signed with the Illinois firm, in April, 1925, a tornado struck in Harrison, Gibson, and Posey counties. Though it wreaked untold disaster, it proved two things—that insurance hereafter would be a necessity on the farm, and that people can always be counted on to respond to human need.

Scores of people were killed, many were injured, and buildings were flattened. Within twelve hours, the Indiana Farm Bureau had opened a relief station at the Gibson County Farm Bureau office in Princeton. Letters were sent to every township and county Farm Bureau and to county agricultural agents asking for financial and material assistance. Jerry East, county agent, and Joe Adams, manager of a local shipping association, joined Farm Bureau people to clear the land of debris and to plow and plant. Three carloads of supplies came. Sears

Roebuck and Company through radio time raised
$1,000 to help. Manufacturers sent tractors, plows,
and other implements to be used in the work. Thirty
tractors went into operation. More than a hundred
students from Oakland City College volunteered
their services. Evansville College with only a hundred students raised $40,000—more than was really
needed at the time. The surplus went toward building a schoolhouse in the area, long referred to as
the Farm Bureau school. Farm Bureau accepted
into membership free of charge all tornado victims.

While this disaster was fresh in farmers' minds,
the contract with State Farm was signed, an arrangement continued for ten years. At that time a difference of opinion arose over administration. H. R.
Nevins, who had been Morgan county president
and had assisted in state organization work, was
named to head the new insurance operation.

Settle's tenure paralleled the most difficult years
experienced by the Indiana Farm Bureau, not from
anything lacking in his leadership, however. Grain
marketing activities were having great difficulty. The
onion exchange quit business. The Canning Crops
Association and the canning factories were disbanded, the Indiana Farm Bureau purchasing
department quit with a large deficit.

Because of these difficulties, which were no more
than farmers painfully learning the rules of business,
membership in the organization suffered. When
commercial ventures, in which farmers had held

high hopes, had not come up to expectations, the membership declined. In 1933, it hit an all-time low of 23,000 and rallied only slowly until after 1940.

After Settle's defeat for re-election to the Indiana Farm Bureau presidency by Lewis Taylor, he turned his energies elsewhere. He was not one to "sulk in his tent." He enlisted in the causes of the national Democratic party, serving first as chairman of the All-party Roosevelt Agriculture Committee during Franklin Delano Roosevelt's campaign for re-election in 1936. He later served with the United States Department of Agriculture in the administration of the Agricultural Adjustment Act.

"Civil War" Year

The insurance business, launched under contract with the Illinois company, grew rapidly. Commissions from it poured into the Indiana Farm Bureau treasury more than $30,000 annually. This the leaders liked because of the organization's straitened circumstances.

But preliminary surveys made by Indiana Farm Bureau Co-operative Association leaders determined in the early thirties that farmers, to their own advantage, could establish a farmer-owned insurance company. President Settle was firmly against it. He appreciated the certainty of $30,000 annually for the treasury, and could not envision that a Farm Bureau-owned company could do better.

The Co-operative leaders and much of the Farm

Bureau leadership were as sure of its advisability as
Settle was of its risks. The war was on. The show-
down came during the Indiana Farm Bureau 1934
convention in Tomlinson Hall, Indianapolis, details
of which must be told so events that followed may
be understood.

The Indiana Farm Bureau board of directors at
that time contained 16 members, to include one
from each of the affiliated co-operatives. Dissent
over whether to renew the existing insurance contract or to start their own company developed in
board meetings. Feeling was so evenly divided the
FB board decided to leave the decision to the delegates at the next convention.

Anson Thomas was Settle's administrative assistant. As feeling grew for the establishment of a
mutual insurance company, Thomas found himself,
through loyalty to his boss, aligned with Settle.

Sentiment soon reached fever pitch.

Innocent of all this development was one Hassil
E. Schenck, a struggling young Boone county
farmer, whose leadership qualities had already been
recognized by his neighbors. As a member of the
convention rules committee and as his county's Farm
Bureau president, he came to the event in Tomlinson
Hall as ignorant of board dissent as anyone could
possibly have been.

In a prior meeting of the rules committee, Schenck
heard the chairman make a report proposed for the
convention floor. Young Schenck protested:

"But one point there is not in accordance with the by-laws of the organization."

The committee chairman persisted: "But we've been told to present our report this way."

Schenck then asked that he be allowed to make a minority report. His statement before the delegate body, made because he could not agree to a violation of the by-laws, was perhaps responsible for his becoming vice-president and soon afterward president of Indiana's largest general farm organization.

The election of the president hinged upon the insurance issue. Intense feeling preceded the voting. To prevent any physical outbreak, Farm Bureau Co-operative workers were placed at strategic locations among the delegates. A simple majority of votes was necessary for election. When the count of ballots was reported after the first vote, Settle had 64; Taylor, 69; and Maurice Douglas and Schenck, whose names had been injected into the balloting for possible leverage if necessary, had six and 13 respectively.

On a second ballot, Settle received 61; Taylor, 82; Douglas, 4; and Schenck, 5. Settle had been defeated and Taylor elected. Of the four names in the balloting, three belonged to men whose heads were graying. Mr. Schenck was the young man on the scene.

In a surprising move, the delegate body unanimously elected him vice-president, since Taylor's elevation had left that position vacant. Those present had evidently liked what the Boone county leader had to say on the convention floor. He had gained stature through a sincere disagreement based on an honest conviction.

Insurance Business Launched

The contract with the Illinois insurance company had terminated in October prior to the 1934 convention. The first order of business facing newly-elected President Taylor was the forming of a mutual insurance company. He had run on that platform, so to speak.

Thus came into being in February, 1935, the Farm Bureau Mutual Insurance Company of Indiana, Inc., with a contributed surplus of $15,000, licensed to sell automobile insurance coverages.

In the first year, 3,341 policies were sold, although at the end of that period there remained only $148 surplus. Assets amounted to little more than $400. Many, even among members, were skeptical of the new undertaking.

In 1937, under President Schenck and by delegate approval, the Hoosier Farm Bureau Life Insurance Company was established as a legal reserve mutual company under the 1935 Indiana Life Insurance Act. Policy number one was sold to Mr. Schenck. To him as president, the insurance companies' growth became a source of great pride.

Guaranteed surplus contribution certificates totaling $32,410 were sold to individuals, to township and county Farm Bureaus, and to local and State Farm Bureau co-operatives. All have since been repaid.

The life company met ready response. More than 2,000 charter applications amounting to more than $2 million were received—ten times the legal requirement for permission to enter the life insurance field in Indiana. This company has since added to its coverages and now offers insurance against hospital and surgical costs, polio and other specified diseases.

To get a picture of its rate of growth—at the end of the first ten years, it had $47 million face value on lives insured; at the end of 20 years, $181 million; and closed 1967 (30 years) with $601 million. Policy dividends have been an important factor in reducing the cost of life insurance to Hoosier life policyholders.

In 1946, with $100,000 surplus contributed by Farm Bureau members and various affiliated organizations, fire and tornado insurance was issued through a new company, the Farm Bureau Mutual Fire and Tornado Insurance Company. That those interested were willing to raise $100,000 at that time reflected the great confidence the members and affiliated organizations had in the future of Farm Bureau and the insurance companies. Two years later, May 1, 1948, this company merged with the one organized in 1935, to become known as the Farm Bureau Mutual Insurance Company of Indi-

ana. ("Inc." was dropped from the corporate name
at that time.)

The fire and casualty company has made excellent
growth. At the end of 1967, it had assets of $41,-
128,621. Farm Bureau Mutual insures more automobiles, trucks and school buses than any other company domiciled in the state. While the dividends from
the life company are rather stable year after year,
those earned in the fire and casualty company fluctu-
ate according to that year's experience, which is es-
sentially of a short-term nature. Some years are very
profitable and some less so.

In 1953, again Farm Bureau and the insurance
companies united to solve a rising membership problem. Because of a tendency among auto dealers to
offer a "tie-in" with an insurance company and perhaps a lending agency when they sell a car, it had
been suggested that Farm Bureau establish a financing agency. To provide the capital structure for the
Rural Acceptance Corporation, Farm Bureau bought
1,000 shares and Farm Bureau Mutual Insurance
Company bought 10,000 shares of stock at $100 per
share. While initially designed to make loans on
automobiles, this service was expanded in 1959 to

offer loans on farm implements and farm and home improvements. Vance L. Denney was the first manager.

While some counties have Farm Bureau credit unions, many do not; and in some cases, the local credit union does not have ample funds to meet Farm Bureau members' financial needs. The Rural Acceptance Corporation offers its services everywhere in the state.

Until 1954 totally wrecked cars had been sold to salvage dealers on a competitive bid basis. To reduce and better control losses, Ellis Metheny, an insurance company employee, suggested the insurance company set up a salvage yard to handle its total wrecks.

January 1, 1954, Superior Parts, Inc., came into being as a subsidiary of the insurance company. It was operated for a time from acreage acquired in Boone county, until a new highway necessitated relocation. There are now two salvage yards—one near Logansport and one near Bedford—handling approximately 1,200 total wrecks each year. Some parts are used in repairing insured autos; others sold through commercial outlets. The manager from date of organization has been Ralph Emmons.

Both the Rural Acceptance Corporation and Superior Parts are affiliates operated by the Farm Bureau Mutual Insurance Company. These services for farmers are unique.

When the casualty company was launched, most

agents were farmers who worked at selling insurance
on a part-time basis. The original agents could easily
handle the sale of auto policies because there was
but one rate for all in those days. In the early days
of the life company, only a few policies were offered.
But as services expanded and policies were tailored
more to the farmers' needs, the job became more
complicated.

It soon became apparent that highly trained, full-
time agents were necessary if Farm Bureau was to
hold its own in the insurance field. There are now
eight regional sales managers, 62 agency managers,
28 county managers, and 231 agents.

The company developed a pattern of closed
territories for agents which has made the job of selling more attractive to Farm Bureau insurance salesmen and has attracted national attention from other
companies' management.

The insurance companies now have offices
throughout the state. There are seven regional claims
offices to bring service on accidents closer to the
insured. This regional plan of claims service was
another innovation that has been adopted by other
companies.

The IFB companies were also the first to write
farm liability coverage without requiring farmers to
keep farm labor records. This plan was developed
with the assistance of Purdue University leaders who
suggested that liability rates be set on the basis of

the number of man-work units required to operate the farm.

An outstanding innovation was the development by the companies of a coverage called contingent workmen's compensation. Designed to be sold at a nominal charge as a part of other liability contracts, this insurance is, in effect, an umbrella of coverage to protect the insured who occasionally needs the brief service of a plumber, a carpenter, or the like who could in event of injury claim compensation under the Workmen's Compensation Act.

Before World War II, the first group hospital and surgical insurance for Farm Bureau members was developed. While this plan has been dropped, it spurred the development of the county membership and insurance office, since farmers formed the habit of coming to the Farm Bureau office to pay their premiums. The potential value of the office had been demonstrated in service to Farm Bureau members and insureds.

In 1961 a clever and again another unique feature in Indiana Farm Bureau insurance was developed for the convenience of the insured. Thrifty McBip (the acronym for Monthly Combined Budgeted Insurance Premiums) was introduced, making it possible to pay a uniform monthly premium to cover all insurance policies. A significant number of policyholders have been attracted to the plan with an average of two and one-half policies each.

The soundness of planning by those who helped

develop the companies is supported by the fact that auto rates are generally the best in the state.

It is usually impractical for a fire and casualty company to offer all lines of coverage that may be needed by its thousands of policyholders. In 1959 the Rural Insurance Agency was organized as a wholly owned subsidiary of the Farm Bureau Mutual Insurance Company. It has contracts with other insurance companies for the writing of policies not written by the Farm Bureau companies. In this manner, agents can offer a full line of insurance to all customers. The first manager of RIA was Foster Williams, since succeeded by Ray Beck.

In 1963 and early 1964, the board of directors and management conducted an extensive study to see if there were advantages in converting the life company from a mutual company to a stock company. The advantages outweighed the disadvantages so the board authorized a new life company to be known as the United Farm Bureau Family Life Insurance Company. The new company was developed so that ownership of all outstanding shares of common stock belongs to the Indiana Farm Bureau, Inc., except for qualifying shares required by law to be owned by directors.

At the close of business June 30, 1964, the Hoosier Farm Bureau Life Insurance Company merged with the United Farm Bureau Family Life Insurance Company. The proportionate share of the free surplus of the merging Hoosier company was allocated to each policyholder. The United Farm Bureau Family Life Insurance Company issues participating policies so that policyholders continue to share in savings effected through operations.

January 1, 1966, the Farm Bureau Mutual Insurance Company of Indiana changed its name to United Farm Bureau Mutual Insurance Company. As both companies have the same directors, management, and a combined agency force, it seemed wise to make this change in name.

The first office of the mutual company was in the Lemcke Building at 106 East Market Street (1935-1936). To provide for expansion, the offices were moved to the Old Trails Building at 309 West Washington Street (1936-1941). The next move was to the Majestic Building at 47 South Pennsylvania Street. This building was occupied by the Indiana Farm Bureau Co-operative Association (1941-1945). It soon became too small. The insurance companies moved across the street to the Century Building (1945-1947).

In 1947 the United States government exercised its right of eminent domain taking over the entire building thus forcing another move. From the Century Building, operations were moved to the Union Title Building at 155 East Market Street (1947-1949). Extensive remodeling was done and the companies remained at this location until 1949.

In 1947 the companies and the Indiana Farm Bureau Co-operative Association joined together and formed the Farm Bureau Building Corporation to buy the Meyer-Kiser Security Trust Building at 130 East Washington Street and the Majestic Building at 47 South Pennsylvania Street. Later through agreement the insurance companies acquired one hundred per cent interest in the Meyer-Kiser Building and the co-operative association the entire interest in 47 South Pennsylvania Street.

After the companies moved to 130 East Washington Street (1949), they had an opportunity to buy ground immediately west formerly occupied by the Vonnegut Building. This space was acquired for future expansion. Later ground immediately east became available. In March, 1967, plans were announced to expand on the ground acquired east of the insurance building. The new structure will more than double the facilities adding approximately 125,000 square feet of floor area. To be completed in 1969, the twelve-story addition will provide adequate housing for the insurance companies, Indiana Farm Bureau, Inc., and some affiliated organizations.

In the early years of the insurance company history, management was through the Farm Bureau Intermediate Corporation in which L. L. Needler had a prominent role. The minutes of April 24, 1936, record that L. L. Needler was "by previous resolution delegated as being in charge of the affairs of insurance." The minutes of March 21, 1936, name him as executive director in charge of all insurance work. He was relieved of his insurance responsibilities May 17, 1937, at his own request. The first manager of the casualty operation, technically an employee of the Farm Bureau Intermediate Corporation, was T. Ivan King, who was with the company until his resignation May 25, 1936.

Paul E. Edwards was hired June 19, 1936, for "underwriting work" and Frank E. Lamb was hired to work on claims. Records are not clear on the dissolution of the Intermediate Corporation.

Edwards was appointed general manager of the Farm Bureau Mutual Insurance Company of Indiana on May 17, 1937. When he was called to active military duty in 1942, Lamb became acting general manager. Edwards returned from military duty in 1945 to continue as manager of the casualty company until his resignation January 1, 1947.

Morley Ringer was employed to manage the new life company in May, 1937. When he entered active military duty in 1942, Jack J. Rosebrough was designated acting manager to continue in that capacity until Ringer returned in 1945.

Rosebrough, who had been made manager of the casualty company upon Edwards' resignation January 1, 1947, was given additional responsibility as manager of the life company when Ringer resigned July 1, 1948. Management has since continued under his direction.

Then There Was Light

The story of the development of farm life in the
United States is the story of the development of
freedom. In 1776 freedom was but a dream. Once
the colonists were rid of their British taskmasters,
they turned to the riddance of other oppressive and
impeding forces in their lives.

There were still the gruelling long hours of heavy
physical labor, if a man were to exact a living from
the new land. There were trees to be felled, savages
to be routed, disease to be battled. The farmer was
independent but he was not free.

Exhausted from a day's work, he had little time
or energy to improve his mind at night. A flickering
grease lamp, hung on the back of his favorite rock-
ing chair, was little help. A few thousand farmers in
the whole country could turn over the manual labor
to their slaves. But for the majority, life on the land
was a daily challenge to their strength and their wits.

The load of work became somewhat lighter with
the industrial revolution which brought the reaper,
the plow and the thresher. Mechanized and motorized equipment provided further boon.

But few will deny that the greatest blessing to life
on the farm was the coming of electricity. It was in
1936 that this was made possible on a large scale by
the enactment of a bill in the Indiana General Assembly which authorized the development of the
Rural Electric Membership Cooperatives.

At that time only a little more than 11 per cent of Indiana farmers had electricity. These fortunate ones happened to be residing along the lines of an established utility company. The author's father installed a half-mile of line at his own expense in order to have light and power. I. H. Hull had electricity on his LaPorte county farm in 1922.

The Indiana law set the pattern for national legislation that was to be enacted the same year, 1936. However, in readiness for this growing rural demand for electricity, President Franklin Delano Roosevelt had issued an executive order in 1935 which made money or loans available for building these distribution facilities.

Because of Indiana's pioneering in this field of service to farmers, Boone county in 1935 became the first in the nation to take advantage of this money. Original development work on a broad scale was planned and directed by IFBCA leaders in 1936, working closely with IFB.

I. H. Hull, named first manager of the Indiana Statewide Rural Electric Co-operative, can take great satisfaction in the fact that it may have been his appearance before a U.S. Senate hearing in 1933 which led to the Rural Electrification Administration, established by Congress in 1936. The national lawmakers heard this Hoosier farm leader report on the many co-operative ventures farmers were engaged in in Indiana to protect themselves against high farm supply prices and to get better prices for their products. The hearing concerned the Farm Credit Act, but Senator George Norris of Nebraska, after hearing Hull's story, asked: "Why can't farmers bring electricity to their farms?" An idea was born.

Senator Norris became a vocal advocate of the REA and author of the bill which established the Tennessee Valley Authority.

While some of the REA's opponents yelled "socialism," it must be admitted that it achieved three things of real benefit. It stimulated farm production, it reduced the hard labor that had always been part and parcel of farming, and it made living far more enjoyable.

There were those who were skeptical of the whole venture. They thought the REMC's would never be profitable. If they had that potential, why hadn't the existing utility companies jumped at the opportunity, they asked.

Claude R. Wickard, who had been a township and Carroll County FB president, helped Indiana farmers get loans for their electric lines and poles while he was Secretary of Agriculture. He later was REA administrator.

The question often discussed among today's farmers is one of ownership of the REMC's. In the State Rural Electrification Act, there were two choices for the establishment of ownership of the distribution lines. The Indiana co-ops were incorporated under the one which leaves possession rather vague, though leaders of the day had the advice of legal counsel. Since a number of the REMC's have paid off their federal loans, the question of ownership of equities demands some kind of definitive action.

When organization work started, Hull, Marvin Briggs, and other Farm Bureau leaders found farmers most eager to share in this modern convenience of electricity. The work moved ahead as rapidly as possible. Some of the existing utility companies began to show a change of heart. They had heretofore refused to build the lines into the rural areas, because they deemed such an undertaking unprofitable.

Briggs, who became the second manager of the state electric co-op organization, tells of stepping aside and letting the Northern Indiana Power Company develop the Hamilton county area. Paul Wheeler, who was county president at the time, verifies this. What the farmers wanted above all was electric current on their farms.

The IFBCA had at one time $87,000 invested in organization work for the REMC's, but it was all repaid.

National regulations required that there be a minimum average of three customers per rural mile, before an REA loan could be granted. Such loans were also available to other utility companies that extended lines into farming areas.

Some calculating utility operators were heard to say during this construction period: "We'll soon buy some bargains." But that was never to be.

Once there was the possibility of having electricity on their farms, FB solicitors worked urgently. By the end of 1936, 17 counties had complied with the law, established their co-ops, and had used up the state's maximum allotment of money for the year. The first ten counties to reach their allotments were: Boone, Carroll, Hendricks, Henry, Hancock, Huntington, Johnson, Shelby, Wabash, and Whitley.

By 1937, of the $85 million first appropriated by the Congress for the REA, Indiana had been granted in loans one-fourteenth of the total, and had strung lines to serve 30,000 homes. By 1941, this figure had risen to 50,000. Today more than 99 per cent of Indiana farm homes have electricity, including those served by non-REMC utilities.

The original Indiana law defined territory for the REMC's by allowing them to develop any area not then served by another utility including towns no larger than 1,500 population. To complicate interpretation of that law, growing towns have spread into the suburbs, which were originally rural territory allotted to the rural co-ops. Also, some industries have gone into the country to build new plants. While they exist in REMC territory, they are like tempting fruit dangling just beyond the reach of the competing utility. Over this issue there has been considerable discussion. A 1953 law, however, set the date of the original electric service as the date for determining population and territory.

While these electric co-operatives were stringing taut wires across the rural landscape, raising poles to support them, and opening 42 offices to operate these new businesses, valued in 1966 at more than $76.5 million, the results on the farm had far greater impact than the monetary value indicates. A way of life was on the way out. A new era had arrived.

Kerosene lamps had been put aside for emergency use only. The oil or wood-burning cook stove was tossed onto the junk heap. The broom gave way to the vacuum sweeper. Gradually other conveniences came into the kitchen to mix and beat, toast and broil and fry.

At the barn, hand-turned feed grinders made way for motorized ones. The premises were lighted by that great redeemer from the dark—the electric light bulb. In time, automatic feeding equipment was installed to shift from the shoulders of the farmer the daily job of tossing and toting. Electricity has not only reduced the burden of manual labor on the farm; it has also reduced the number of men needed.

Along with the fuel-propelled tractor, electricity became another boon in the liberation of the farmer.

Under construction near Petersburg in 1967 was a new electric power generating plant being built by a division of Indiana Statewide Rural Electric Co-operative, called Hoosier Energy Division. Several Hoosier REMC's are cooperating to build this plant with an REA loan, and when completed it is expected to provide power to many of the local REMC co-ops.

Though destined only briefly to head the Indiana Farm Bureau, Lewis Taylor's influence was felt from the beginning. While a lecturer for the Farmers' Institutes he had pleaded strongly for a farm organization. He was chairman of the March 25, 1919, meeting held in Indianapolis to arouse interest in such a movement. At the second board meeting, he was named secretary. He later served as treasurer, first vice-president, and head of the tax and legislative committee. He is the only man to have held all four top offices in the IFB.

Mr. Taylor was born June 5, 1864, in Warrick county, Indiana, the son of Hubbard and Nancy Robinette Taylor. He maintained residence on a farm near Newburgh in that county all his life. He attended DePauw University, and was later graduated from Indiana University in 1896.

In 1897, young Taylor went to the gold fields of Alaska to work as manager for an Evansville company, which owned gold mines near Juneau. Though the mining venture was successful, he returned to Indiana two years later and with his brother, Isham Taylor, opened a law office in Evansville. Two years later found him back on his farm, his first love.

His zeal for the cause of agriculture lifted him from one position to another higher one. President

Taylor was once called into conference with President Franklin D. Roosevelt.

This leader's sense of what he deemed right was so firmly fixed that he was not capable of compromise, according to his co-workers; but he learned early in organization work to delegate to others assignments that called for compromise settlement. His gentle and unassuming manner and high hopes colored all that President Taylor said and did. It has been said that he was deserving of FB's highest office 15 years before it came to him. Before becoming president, Taylor was sent by the AFBF into the southern states to do organization work for a time.

As might have been expected, Taylor's greatest interest was in education. In an early address, he said: "Paying for schools is everybody's business . . . eventually money for teachers must come from the state to be administered locally." This came about, in part, but only after death had removed him from the scene.

His intense feeling for the cause of agriculture and his gift with language are reflected in these words which he wrote for The HOOSIER FARMER in 1935:

"The farmer who does not support this program . . . definitely lines up with the enemies of agriculture . . . the packers, the handlers, and the processors who have fattened at his crib for generations . . . Indiana agriculture needs men not afraid to pluck

the beards of the lords of the money changers who
rob them of their hard earned dollars,—men who
will dare to strike political plunderers from public
office . . . farm men not afraid to break a lance for
the farm family and the farm home."

Taylor's short tenure as president was marked
by the formation of the mutual casualty insurance
company, which proved to be the groundwork for a
multi-million dollar business. He saw the beginning
of the electric age on the farm; and he had been
influential in the passage of Indiana's Gross Income
Tax Law.

A Farm Bureau-sponsored trip to Pasadena,
California, in 1936 for the annual convention of the
American Farm Bureau, attended by President and
Mrs. Taylor, and 145 other Hoosiers proved to be
too much for the Indiana leader. He died there of
a heart attack. Vice-President and Mrs. Hassil E.
Schenck accompanied Mrs. Taylor on her sad
return to the hills of southern Indiana with the body
of her husband.

+

Chapter IV
Years of Travail

+

Financial Difficulties

During the first 20 years of the organization's history, state leaders were having as much difficulty in financing the stripling Farm Bureau as its members were having in financing their farming operations. Those were hard times. Farm Bureau membership was not yet established in size as it is today. It fluctuated with every turn of events. It must also be remembered that in 1932, it took 50 dozen eggs to pay the membership dues for a year.

Some trial efforts in the commercial field were destined to fail because they were being directed by men unschooled in business. And every disappointment acted as a damper on membership. Since the annual dues were then the only source of income, and the program was from the first large in scope, there was disparity between the supply and the demand for money.

During the first months of organization, leaders had frantically tried different plans to replenish the treasury. They suggested a levy on each farm in the state, whether the owner belonged to Farm Bureau or not. Every farmer would benefit, and Farm Bureau was for all farmers, it was argued.

They also asked each county to pay an assessment of $200 while the members were being enlisted. This plan served to give the state office operating funds for a time. At the first convention of the Indiana Farm Bureau, Treasurer Charles G. Chester of

Lake county reported a balance of $14,729.92.

Many counties had Better Farming Associations which extension leaders had encouraged. When L. E. Hoffman, later to become state director of the Purdue Extension Service, went to Jay County as agricultural agent, he found they already had a BFA. Soon after his arrival there in May, 1919, a state organizer came to the area to ask that group to become a member of the new Indiana Federation of Farmers' Associations. To do so, they were told they would be required to pay $200 into the state organization's treasury.

The solicitor was in a hurry to catch the returning interurban car to Indianapolis. There were forty men present at the called meeting. That meant $5 each. Harry Fennig, who was to become the first county Farm Bureau president, suggested they go along with the man's suggestion. Others agreed. To save time, Fennig wrote his personal check for $200. Check in hand, Hoffman raced to the interurban station to catch the departing solicitor just before he responded to the "All aboard!"

Staff members and officers worked day and night to stretch their energies over the needs of the burgeoning program, in order to meet the expectations of the members. The leaders' belief in the eventual success of the undertaking transformed their arduous schedule into a labor of love. But even then, it was a kind of hand-to-mouth existence from year to year.

During Settle's tenure, he even resorted to trying

to sell fire extinguishers to raise money. He bought a carload of the devices and proposed that the women sell them. Mrs. Sewell, who then headed the women's department, said "No; let's get to work and enroll more members." According to Larry Brandon, "Those fire extinguishers rusted out in wagon sheds all over the state."

During this early period, the parent had to turn frequently to the offspring, the Indiana Farm Bureau Co-operative Association, for a loan. While the purchasing department had been dropped from the IFB because it was financially unsuccessful, the re-organized supply co-op was born a-running, or so it seems. It was soon in a position to help the membership organization.

When Hassil E. Schenck became president in 1936 upon the death of Lewis Taylor, he learned that the state Co-op had forwarded $6,000 to help meet the IFB payroll. As membership dues were forwarded to the state office, the loan was repaid; but another $10,000 had to be borrowed from the same source later.

As president, early in 1937, Schenck decided that the balance sheet needed special attention. He called in all employees who were then receiving more than $3,000 per year, and asked them to join him in taking an automatic reduction to three thousand until the budget could be balanced. Staff members agreed to the plan, and there was no more borrowing for operating expenses thereafter.

Down through the years, management and boards of directors of the many Farm Bureau-affiliated organizations have considered it wise to support IFB programs that dovetail with their interests.

In 1937, Larry Brandon, who had been second district director, came to the state office as organization director, vice-president and secretary-treasurer. At that time the membership stood at 29,000. Three of the five dollar membership dues were being held in the county and township.

As soon as he was able to assess the immense task that faced him, Brandon began to urge increased dues. He says that he was frustrated by lack of money and personnel and "threatened to quit every weekend when I went to my home in DeKalb county." By 1945 the membership had risen to 50,000.

President Schenck saw that there was a definite need for more money in the treasury. But it was not until 1948 that the dues were doubled to $10. Nineteen years later—in 1967—they were raised to $15 to finance an expanded program.

The result is a surplus large enough to assure the organization's permanence. There was to be no more of this business of not being able to meet a payroll, or not being able to hold onto good employees capable of making the program a success.

Presently, of the $15 dues, $6.75 remains in the county, $6.75 goes to the IFB treasury, and $1.50 is forwarded to the American Farm Bureau Federation.

State leaders husband the resources well. The treasurer's report as given to the 1967 convention showed total assets of more than $2 million. Most of this money is invested in U.S. Savings and Treasury bonds, and interest-bearing investments in affiliated organizations.

In the early thirties, farmers established credit unions in 46 counties. By their charters, all members of FB, the county FB co-op, and all members of their families are eligible to borrow money. A state Co-op bank at Beech Grove was established as a repository for surplus funds from the county or a source of financial aid for the credit unions. It did not develop into the role expected of it, because it did not become large enough to handle the counties' growing needs; so it was sold in 1953.

Farm Bureau and Partisan Politics

The Indiana Farm Bureau leadership has always been able to walk a tight rope when it came to partisan politics. It was an issue hotly debated in the beginning. While it was most desirable that members participate in local or state government, if they were to have their interests fairly represented, the organization itself could not take sides politically.

It should here be noted that other groups that have not been so successful in maintaining political bipartisanship have found themselves married for life, in the public mind, to one or the other of the major parties.

By shaping policies to meet issues rather than to conform to some political philosophy, it has been possible at times to win support from both parties at the same time, in both state and national legislative bodies. If some candidate had been openly supported because he agreed with FB policies, the Indiana Farm Bureau would have been accused by a rival office seeker of playing politics.

This neutral policy has of course left many disappointed candidates in its wake. It is also true that candidates frequently try to hitch their wagon to FB. On the other hand, many politicians, when not seeking office, have openly championed the organization.

The late Henry Schricker, Knox, Indiana, twice elected Governor of the state, helped organize Oregon township, Starke county, Farm Bureau and was a loyal friend to the end.

In the early days of Farm Bureau, before this non-partisan policy had been defined, a Marion

County farmer, William Bosson, who was serving as secretary of the IFB executive committee and a special treasurer, was asked to manage the Indiana campaign of Illinois Governor Frank Lowden in his pursuit of the nomination for President of the United States. This was an honor not to be taken lightly. Bosson planned to accept the offer. The political action question then came to a head.

The board of directors passed a resolution in February, 1920, which said: "Any state officer or director of this organization in courtesy to the Indiana Federation of Farmers' Associations, before entering into politics as a candidate or as a candidate's manager, (should) resign his official position with the said IFFA."

Bosson resigned, but there have been others since that time who sought office and, because they were not elected, did not resign.

Since state leaders emphasize the need for farmers to be active in politics, there has always been some response to the suggestion. Earl Crawford, sixth district director from Wayne county, resigned in 1921 to accept a post on the State Highway Commission. John J. Brown, ninth district director from Spencer county (and not to be confused with President John G. Brown) was chairman of the Board of State Tax Commissioners.

Maurice Douglas, who was vice-president of the IFB, became a member of the Public Service Commission, and then a state senator. In that role, he introduced Farm Bureau's first sponsored bill. Later he was elected director of the IFB from the eighth district.

Other FB directors who held public office were C. R. Benjamin, Lake county, who was named one of the state Tax Commissioners; and Howard Atcheson, Scott county, tenth district director, who was appointed to the State Highway Commission. Both first resigned as IFB directors.

M. Clifford Townsend, who had been FB state organization director for three years, was elected Lieutenant Governor of Indiana in 1932, then Governor in the next election in 1936. C. S. Masterson was made director of the state's rural fire department. L. L. Needler, who had been a fourth district director and later a staff member of the state organization, became state purchasing agent under Governor Townsend.

Maurice Hanson, once Steuben county president, became a state senator, as did Oliver Cannon. I. H. Hull and C. E. Moseley, long time FB and IFBCA directors, served in the Indiana House of Representatives.

Claude Wickard, the first president of his township FB and later Carroll county president, rose from the state legislature to national responsibilities. He was a member of the Indiana Senate when FB members in 1932 made their first march on the State House to demand property tax relief from a special session of the General Assembly.

"It was a bit frightening," Wickard recalled, as he was on the inside looking out, so to speak; but the press never referred to the mass action as a show of violence.

Wickard's leadership qualities were recognized through his activities in the AAA corn-hog program at state and regional levels, during the Depression. Then he was appointed Under Secretary, then Secretary of Agriculture under Franklin D. Roosevelt, and REA Administrator under President Harry S. Truman.

Mrs. Wickard enjoyed telling of his refusal, at first, to accept Washington responsibility, because it was oats harvesting time.

"Oats were then selling for seven cents a bushel." she chided.

But Wickard's first allegiance was to his neighbors, whose oats he had promised to thresh with his equipment. Not until the oats were harvested, did this Carroll county farm leader assume his larger role in the nation's capital.

A seventh district FB director, Clarence McCormick of Knox county, also had a national role as Under Secretary of Agriculture under President Truman.

Mrs. Claude Crooks, fifth district woman leader from Parke county, and former IFB president, Hassil E. Schenck, each served on appointment by the Governor as trustee of Purdue University. Schenck also was a member of the national agricultural advisory committee under President Dwight D. Eisenhower, an honor later held by Wickard under President John F. Kennedy.

Marvin Briggs in 1964 completed ten years of service on the Federal Farm Credit Board. This was the longest tenure ever held by one man on that Board. James K. Mason, eighth district IFB director, preceded Briggs in that position.

The first women's department head, Mrs. Ed Hatch of Allen county, was faced with the decision of whether to resign or refuse a political assignment. She did resign and became active in Al Smith's Indiana campaign for President of the U.S.

The increasing number of farmers in state government in the early twenties, and their insistence through Farm Bureau that action be taken to correct conditions unfair to them, caused the 1923 Assembly to be tagged as "the farmers' legislature." Until that time, while farmers cast about half the votes in the state, they had had only weak representation in the General Assembly.

Many have served in various capacities in government who are not here listed. Anson Thomas for many years was a member of and chairman of several important state commissions. He was repeatedly lauded and honored for his work in the Assembly as Farm Bureau's legislative director.

Many farmers have served as county officials and township trustees. All these men (and women) have proved that good government is a primary concern of farmers. The organization has also proved that to be most effective, it is advisable to stick to issues.

Above and Beyond

Many Farm Bureau leaders at the local level have given their all to the cause of equality for agriculture. Untold hours, after the day's work was done, have been spent in attending meetings to manage organizational business, in making talks before their own and other groups, in advising Rural Youth and 4-H groups. They have sought their neighbors' membership and defended FB policies.

Without these local people, the organization would have died. We cannot name these persons individually because of space limitations, but the glory is theirs. They have made it possible for the state and national FB program to move forward.

There are a few persons at the state level, whose efforts above and beyond the duties of their offices, call for commendation. At the risk of offending some, let us name a few.

The presidents, who found themselves in the top role because they had indicated an eagerness and zeal for the cause, are discussed elsewhere.

Larry Brandon cannot be passed by without tribute to his untiring efforts. Born into a home where it was not the custom to attend chuch services, Larry found a new life when he married the daughter

Above and Beyond

(Above): The evangelism of I. H. Hull, left, and Larry Brandon was a potent factor in the early history of Farm Bureau.

(Center): The practical sense and hard work of Anson Thomas (Left): Scott Meiks, and Marvin Briggs (below) helped to build strong Farm Bureau organizations.

(Above): Modern county Farm Bureau and Insurance offices like this one in Wabash county serve members in every county as headquarters for membership and insurance service.

(Below): Gateway to state FB headquarters on the 11th floor of the FB Insurance Building in Indianapolis is this inviting lobby which gives farmers ready access to state leaders.

(Right): In earlier times (1938) FB, Co-op and Insurance agents all served farmers from the same building like the Whitley county center.

Modern
Affiliate

Management
Team

Jack J. Rosebrough
Executive Vice-President
Farm Bureau Insurance

Harold P. Jordan
General Manager
Indiana Farm Bureau Cooperative
Association, Inc.

W. R. Cummins
General Manager
Producers Marketing Association

(Above): Trucks and cars are shown at the Indianapolis Stock Yards in 1923. Producers Marketing Association was new but very prominent there even at that early date.

(Below): Crowd of Boone county farmers and visitors watch the raising of the first R.E.M.C. pole there on January 9, 1936. The Boone county co-op was the first in the nation to be energized.

of a Civil War veteran who was also a minister of the gospel.

"Our home became a preacher's home, and I learned there is something more to life than just living," he explains.

This adult 'conversion' became a driving force in his young manhood which carried over into everything he did. Equality for agriculture took on, for him, spiritual overtones. He saw in the church, the home, the school, and Farm Bureau a kind of holy alliance that would work for man's improvement. This same zeal also became infectious among several workers in co-operative endeavors in the early days.

But it became Brandon's role to evangelize the state's farmers. He could and often did bring his listeners to tears as he appealed for their help. Through his work, FB audiences came to think of the church and FB as dedicated to the same goal. Brandon employed the fire of a Billy Sunday and the persistence of the modern Billy Graham, yet there was none of the charlatan in him. His listeners went home rededicated to the idea that membership in the Farm Bureau was a moral mandate, like belonging to church.

To this day, Brandon believes that those first small meetings of farmers over the nation prior to the organization of FB were "nothing short of providential." The telling effects of this leader's fire and dedication began to show in an increased membership.

Totals climbed. In 1952, membership passed the 100,000 mark for the first time, and today stands second in the nation while being the second smallest state geographically west of the Allegheny Mountains. (Hawaii is the smallest.) Membership in 1967 topped 153,000.

In the 16 years Brandon was state organization director, on the coldest nights and the hottest days, he traveled more than a half million miles over the state, preaching the Farm Bureau gospel. There has not been another like him.

Although I. H. Hull has been mentioned in other connections, he too, was a dedicated person. After first efforts in the membership organization as county worker then as district director, he became a student and devotee of the co-operative philosophy. Few Indiana farmers have not heard his enlightening talks on the development of the IFB co-operatives and what they have meant to the farmer's welfare. His zeal never waned.

Hull's studies took him to Scandinavia, where he learned that those farmers were far ahead of the U.S. in these self-help programs. His part in setting up the Indiana co-ops on the Rochdale plan, as demonstrated among British weavers—one member, one vote—was insurance of their remaining in farmer control.

Hull and Marvin Briggs, who in 1946 was to

follow him as manager of the IFBCA, traveled many miles over the state selling the idea of Farm Bureau; and later the need for electric co-operatives. Neither received any extra pay for their labors. At first, they sold FB memberships in the wintertime, and tilled the fields in the summer. After Hull became IFBCA's first manager, he hired Briggs in 1927 as the treasurer. Nineteen years later Briggs became the manager, and the man who met the most pressing need of the Co-op at that juncture—which was financial stability equal to its rapidly growing business.

Briggs' training had hardly prepared him for his new responsibility, except for the fact that he had grown up on a farm. He had two years' study in pre-law at Indiana University then decided that law was not for him. He returned to the farm, became a partner with his father and started reading all the agricultural information issued by Purdue. Later Purdue hired him as a member of the Institute staff for five years.

It was in Institute work that he met Mrs. Lewis Taylor, also an instructor, who in turn recommended young Briggs to her husband. This contact led to Briggs' long service in Farm Bureau and the Co-op.

Anson S. Thomas, who played a number of different roles in FB, is another of those who served over and beyond what was required of him. He worked during the difficult years when the organization was understaffed and perhaps underpaid. Night after night, he drove over country roads to explain to members what legislative problems faced the organization, and what they could do to ease the problem of executing FB policies.

Anyone who works all day, then extends himself till midnight hours to make sure the people "get the word," has to feed on dedication to the cause. Such a man was Thomas, who even five years beyond his retirement served by participating in several state commissions whose work directly affects farmers.

In the performance of his duties and the application of a rare portion of common sense, he became one of the best informed persons in the state in the function and nature of state government. From the time when he was a township trustee in Montgomery county until the end of his 31 years service, lastly as lobbyist in the General Assembly, he was learning. He became acquainted with important people; he acquired a liberal knowledge of what government can and should do; and he perfected the art of compromise, so necessary to legislative work.

Chapter V
Other Ventures

Printing Corporation

So firmly convinced were the founders of the Indiana Federation of Farmers' Associations that the printed word would be handmaiden to their success, they contracted as early as May, 1919, for the printing of "no less than 25,000 copies" of their official magazine. Total subscriptions collected were to be turned over to the publisher until the costs were met; another 25,000 were to be bought at actual cost, (we assume, if the additional ones were needed.)

This order was given the printer when there was no certainty that the farm organization would become a reality. In other words, this act alone gives us a glimpse of the faith of the pioneer organizers. They never stopped to question, only to plan.

The Indiana Farm Bureau (IFFA) found its monthly printing needs, including and beyond the magazine, increasing as the program developed. After all, a shortage of state employes could be compensated for by printed information, mailed or distributed to members. There seemed no way but to pay thousands of dollars annually to independent printers.

Then in 1943 the printing plant owned by Samuel R. Guard & Company, Inc., at Spencer, Indiana, was offered for sale in bankruptcy proceedings. Indiana Farm Bureau, Indiana Farm Bureau Co-operative Association, and Farm Bureau Mutual Insurance

Company of Indiana invested equally in the purchase of the plant. The name was changed to Farm
Bureau Printing Corporation.

It was originally set up under the co-operative
laws of the state, but in 1950, when it had become
evident that it could not function as a co-op, it was
reincorporated as a business for profit. The same
three companies owned the property.

Later, it was developed chiefly as a printer of
periodicals, with 16 publications included besides
The HOOSIER FARMER, also the Ohio and West
Virginia Farm Bureau official publications. The
original manager for most of 1943 was Henry C.
Bucher, to be followed by Walter S. Goldberg of
Spencer, who very ably served in that capacity until
the company was sold in 1965.

Hoosier Travel Service

Indicative of the widening horizon of farm people
was the ready acceptance of services offered by
Hoosier Travel Service, incorporated as an affiliate
of IFB in the spring of 1948. Trips to national conventions by rail had opened the eyes of leaders to
the possibility of saving farmers money on travel
costs if they had their own company.

Stock was issued for operating capital and bought
by members of the Indiana Farm Bureau's board of
directors.

Some 7,000 persons took advantage of educational tours conducted by Hoosier Travel to many

parts of the North American continent, to the Holy
Land, to Europe, Hawaii, Japan, Hong Kong, New
Zealand, Australia, and Central and South America.

Glenn W. Sample's vision and leadership in spear-
heading the growth of the Travel Service completely
broke the bonds of provincialism for those persons
who have taken advantage of it. These seven thousand travelers became better informed and more
sophisticated from their experiences.

Those experiences are also very revealing. One
farm woman stopping in a metropolitan hotel on a
tour did not leave her housekeeping habits behind
her. When the hotel management asked why they
hadn't used their room, it was learned she had risen
early, made the bed, repacked their clothes and
stashed the baggage out of sight in a closet, and
cleaned the bathroom, like any good housekeeper
would do. By next night, she had caught on to the
ways of hotel living.

Surprisingly, it has also been noted that some
take a trip abroad without the slightest conception
of where they are on the globe. Also that shift from
one's home community, within a very short time by
modern aircraft, to foreign shores brings with it a
shock from seeing so many foreigners. So the many
people, who traveled for the first time in their lives
because their own farm organization offered to
arrange and escort them at reasonable prices, have
really had an educational experience.

Because of changes in traveling habits of farmers

and in operation of transportation companies, and because of the pressing need for concentrating personnel and resources on other parts of the expanding Farm Bureau program, the Travel Service was discontinued as an organization affiliate and sold to an independent operator in 1966. However, Farm Bureau continues to sponsor tours for rural people when need and interest warrant it.

A recent statement by a television personality that "Today's farmer is less provincial and more sophisticated that the city-born city dweller" is a true reflection of the expanding interests of the people on the land.

P. and C. Food Stores

Farmers have not been able to this day to understand or even to accept the wide margin that exists between the prices paid them for products grown on the farm and the prices they have to pay when they go to the supermarket to buy it back, sometimes in processed form.

In 1946, the Indiana Farm Bureau board of directors decided to try to correct this situation. They opened three co-operative food stores, known as Producers' & Consumers' Family Food Stores, in Lebanon, Greensburg, and Veedersburg. The voting stock in this enterprise was bought by the IFB, the Indiana Farm Bureau Co-operative Association, and Producers Marketing Association. Local farmers and co-ops bought the non-voting, preferred stock.

It all happened at a time when modern super-markets of chain grocery companies were expanding rapidly. Keen competition meant very narrow margins of profit. This in turn meant that volume was necessary if a store were to succeed. Farmers lost interest when they saw they could not compete, and the stores were closed. It should be noted, however, that no individual investor (non-voting stock) lost money in the venture.

The late Hal Royce, who had been director of the livestock department of the Indiana Farm Bureau, was manager of the farmers' trial run in the food business.

Chapter VI
Influence in State Legislature

Learning to Lobby

L aw has long been the first resort of civilized man. Back in the eighteenth century, Samuel Johnson said: "The law is the last result of human wisdom acting upon human experience for the benefit of the public."

Early in its history, the Indiana Federation of Farmers' Associations turned to the state's law-making body to get relief from some of the farmers' most pressing problems. That dependence has been an important factor in the Indiana Farm Bureau development. The resulting volume of laws that has come through this dependence, and the co-operation of legislators, has provided aid of a very permanent nature in public sanitation, human and animal health, equitable taxation, and better schools.

The Farm Bureau image in the Indiana legislature was projected originally in a successful campaign to enact a law permitting interurban cars to haul livestock to the capital city and its terminal market.

"The very idea! Just what you could expect from a bunch of farmers."

These and other such caustic comments came from town and city residents, past whose homes the interurban line ran. Although livestock was already coming to market by railroad and truck, freight costs would be lower by interurban.

Although the urban communities wanted meat on their tables, the idea of bringing it alive via interurban past their very own homes was offensive to their sensitive nostrils.

But the Assemblymen voted with the farmers and the Act became the first Farm Bureau-sponsored bill. The year was 1921.

Lobbying skill had to be acquired by FB leaders. In the fall of 1920, the organization laid its first plans for a tax and legislative campaign in the 1921 session. Since policy development had not had time to come to life, President John G. Brown appointed a committee of five to draft a program. Those five were: Earl Crawford, Russell Van Hook, A. E. Myers, H. E. Lochry, and Everett McClure.

Their proposals called for broadening the tax base and practicing strict economy in state government.

Since Indiana had become the dumping ground for inferior seeds, FB worked successfully for a bill which established certain standards for seeds, to certify their purity. Whole clover crops had been lost in the past because of bad seed that had been pouring into the state.

Bills passed always reflected the times. In those days, the elementary school was usually close by, not far from the pupils' homes; but the high school was more remote and transportation of pupils was a problem. So the General Assembly passed a bill which provided that all rural high school pupils would be hauled.

The State Sanitary Board, which later became the Livestock Sanitary Board, was reorganized to include three farmers and two veterinarians. In 1947, it was enlarged to seven, including four farmers.

In 1922, the IFB board of directors named a committee to handle the legislative program during the '23 session. James Riggs, Sullivan county, was named chairman. Helping him were: T. I. Ferris, Steuben county; Marion Elliott, Decatur; and Walter Baker, Marshall.

The following January 15, there occurred the first meeting of agricultural representatives and state senators. This seems strange in view of the fact that half the popular vote at the time was cast in rural areas. But the state legislators were aware that a new rural force was developing with which they would have to reckon.

This new-found recognition was responsible for the epithet given that session—the "farmers' legislature." But the farmers did not wince. In fact they were aware of a new kind of pride. At last they were making themselves heard.

Reviews of Hard-Won Laws

In the 1923 session, a two-cent tax on gasoline was levied by law, but it exempted non-highway-used fuel. The license on heavy transport trucks was also raised from $75 to $175 per year. These two Acts reflect the growing concern over road maintenance.

Another Act passed in the same session permitted counties to increase assistance to county agents to $1,000 per year. Still another reduced attorney fees on large ditches from four per cent to one per cent of the cost of the ditch. The co-op marketing bill, spearheaded by Assemblyman I. H. Hull, was stopped in one session by middlemen and Indianapolis newspapers, to be passed later in 1925.

Farm Bureau was also successful in getting freight rates on limestone reduced to the level of those charged on crushed stone from quarries within the state.

Another very important bill, while not instigated by farmers, was to serve as a watchdog over local government in the years to come. It allowed the State Board of Accounts to go into townships and counties to investigate official contracts. While this is not used except in cases of glaring irregularities, it serves as a Damoclean sword over the heads of local government office holders.

In characterizing the business of lobbying, Anson Thomas says that to be effective the lobbyist must be "honest, frank, and fair; and he must keep his promises."

All legislation is the result of compromise, with one exception. "The only bill to come through whole is the salary bill," according to this friend of the farmer and veteran habitue of the State House.

If a FB-sponsored bill goes through too many changes, it sometimes becomes necessary to disclaim

it. Long tenure of the Bureau representative in the
state Capitol is desirable, according to Anson.

Through all his years of service in that role, he
held forth at his 'office' (a card table set up in a
corridor) where he was constanly being sought out
for advice on how the Farm Bureau stood on an
issue currently being considered.

It is impossible here to list all the organization's
achievements in the legislature which, though not
wholly creditable to FB, do reflect its growing
prestige.

In 1925, the General Assembly set up procedures
for compulsory testing of cattle for tuberculosis.
This Act removed a grave hazard to human health,
farm and non-farm. A survey which revealed that
farm land was being assessed for taxation at 21
per cent more than its actual cash value led to a bill
which gave the State Tax Board the authority to
reduce assessments horizontally or within any taxing
unit. Another enactment made it unlawful for local
officials to spend more money than they received
from taxes.

It is significant, that in the 1927 session not a
single bill passed that was opposed by Farm Bureau;
and every one sponsored by the organization went
through with flying colors. This singular success led
to the establishment of a tax and legislative department in the state farm organization, with Lewis
Taylor, vice-president, as its director.

By 1931 the national financial crisis was becoming most acute. The authority of the State Board of Health to condemn school buildings not meeting specifications, thus necessitating new ones, was aggravating the tax load on the farmers, since most of those schools that were being condemned were country schools. To relieve the situation, the General Assembly that year froze the state budget, relieved the Board of Health of its authority to force the building of new school houses, and passed an Act providing state aid for schools. That was the year that 1,000 farmers were invited to the Capitol to counsel with the legislators, and the session brought results.

By 1932, the depth of the Great Depression, still more relief was needed from property tax. Forty-thousand farmers, whose names appeared on a petition, asked the Governor to call a special session to take action on their problem. The session was called and a tax limitation law was passed setting a maximum of $1.50 per hundred dollars valuation on real property to finance county budgets. This relief for that one year alone has been estimated at $30 million.

In the same special session, another bill became law which, by formula, divided state highway funds among counties, towns, and cities for road construction and maintenance, and removed this cost from property. The plan was agreed upon about midnight during the session, according to Thomas, after a long and heated discussion with representatives of the petroleum companies, gasoline dealers, trucking firms, and Farm Bureau all taking part in shaping the provisions of the bill.

In recalling the battle that generated so much heat in these talks that night, Thomas smiled and said: "Sometimes the fight is more exciting than the settlement."

The formula spelled out in that Act gives to cities and towns 15 per cent of gasoline tax collections; counties, 32 per cent; and the State Highway Department, 53 per cent. This division remains the same today.

Credit for the Indiana Gross Income Tax law, passed in 1933, goes to Lewis Taylor who labored long in its behalf. Co-operative and REMC laws have been helpful to their growth. Special relief legislation during the difficult years of the thirties saved many a farmer from bankruptcy. Outlawing of the three-mile gravel road bonds for all time was a great boon in 1937.

Ten thousand farmers marched on the State House in 1939 to demand that the Gross Income Tax law, being threatened by a bill to repeal, remain unchanged.

Farm Bureau has traditionally been on the side of keeping legalized betting out of the state and of prohibiting the sale of alcoholic beverages at the Indiana State Fair.

Such practical matters as indemnity for Bangs-diseased cattle that must be destroyed, the reforestation of strip mine areas in the southern part of the state, drainage laws, and insurance laws protecting the policyholder have been supported by Farm Bureau.

A law, in which Thomas takes particular pride, is that which when enacted in 1953 brought into the state treasury from the counties the Common School Fund, a sum which came originally from the sale of land originally granted, but not used, for school purposes. The fund had grown in size and had been historically loaned by county auditors at their own discretion.

The Farm Bureau-sponsored law required that such funds, as fast as they could be collected, be sent to the state treasurer every five months.

"Veteran lawmakers said it could not be done," reports Thomas. But it was. This meant an additional $40 million immediately and $2 millon more each year until all the outstanding loans were collected. Some state officials saw in this a veritable bonanza. They immediately started plans for a new state office building, but common sense won out. The schools were in dire straits, so the money went into a school building loan fund for districts considered to be hardship cases.

In 1953, an outbreak of a virulent swine disease called Viscular Exanthema led to its source—uncooked garbage—and resulted in the passage of legislation which mandated that all commercial garbage be cooked before being fed to hogs. An REMC law in the same session cleared the air on the definition of territory in expanding towns that had grown beyond the original limit of 1,500 population, —as defined by law and granted to REMC's when electricity was brought to them by the co-op. The 1953 law said the determining population shall be its size when electric service first came to the town. Since the original Act gave service of unserved towns up to and including 1,500 people to the REMC, the '53 Act established the co-op's right to continue serving them. Suburban developments and the movement of some industry to rural areas could have been a luscious plum for competing utilities, some of whom were already attempting to move into such disputed terrirtories.

In 1957, on the third attempt, Farm Bureau succeeded in getting a law passed which established a school of veterinary medicine at Purdue University, —a move deemed necessary for adequate livestock care on Indiana farms, and for public health.

Basic revisions in the property tax structure of the state were spelled out in bills which were the culmination of 20 years of work by the tax and legislative department of the Indiana Farm Bureau, at the insistence of the delegate body which year after year had asked that something be done to correct inequities.

The new laws established a manual to guide local assessors; set the assessment value of real estate and personal property at one-third its market value; called for a statewide reassessment of real estate starting with 1962 and every six years thereafter; and provided that school buildings and church properties be required to file for tax exemption every four years to make sure that, if they had been turned to other and profitable uses, they would be added to the tax rolls.

While many of these laws did not directly put money in the farmer's pocket, they have contributed to a climate conducive to an improved standard of living on the farm, and indirectly to more profitable farming.

Taxes and schools continue to be of first concern among FB members. And it is heartening to note that while the farm population has dwindled in Indiana, Farm Bureau's prestige in state government has gained.

Deliberate in reaching a decision; and hard to budge, once he had. That was Hassil E. Schenck, president of the Indiana Farm Bureau from 1937 through 1957, 21 years during which the organization became financially strong and with the membership growing. The frugality he practiced in his own life, he applied to the operation of the FB.

His personal strength came from his unquestioned honesty and what he considered to be morally right.

Born in Boone county where he still resides, he attended elementary school, then four years in Lebanon High School seven miles away. During nice weather he rode a non-coaster type bicycle over this daily distance; in bad weather he drove a horse.

After that he enrolled in two spring terms at Central Normal College at Danville and received some teacher training. For 16 years he taught in a country school, all eight grades, and in that period acquired many of the characteristics of leadership which later stood him in good stead. In the school room, he had become adept at explaining and persuading.

Schenck has been interested in Farm Bureau since the beginning. He was a township vice-president, county vice-president and county president before being elected state vice-president in 1934. He has taught a Sunday school class in the Milledgeville Methodist Church near his home for a longer period than he was IFB president.

When Schenck became state vice-president, he had no plans to spend time away from his farming operation. He had started as a renter, and there was still much work to be done on his expanding acreage. But Taylor's illness and hospitalization almost immediately after his assuming office and lasting through the 1935 General Assembly made it necessary that Schenck act as president during that time.

"I had never presided over any group larger than a local Co-op board or a committee meeting," he said in recalling his trepidation at these new responsibilities which had been thrust upon him.

Those around him were soon to know that this young man had real qualities of leadership. He refused to fire Anson Thomas, who had taken up the cudgel on the side of his employer, President Settle, in the insurance fight. There were those who not only expected him to let Thomas go but insisted that he do it. But Schenck reasoned with clarity that the cleavage over the insurance issue could easily become permanently damaging if all was not forgotten and forgiven.

President Schneck was always fair in his relationship with his employees, though he demanded the best they had to give at all times. The example he set in putting in a full day often had many of his co-workers "hanging onto the ropes." After going to his farm home at the end of a day at the office, during harvest season, he would frequently take his place alongside the hired man on the job.

The author heard him give a very pointed talk on the value of work, before a group of visiting South American agricultural leaders. As is generally known and as he knew from a trip to South America, farm work there is seldom done by the land owner. President Schenck told the visitors of the contribution that manual labor had made to the building of our nation.

To prove his point, he told them: "When I go
home this afternoon, I will change my clothes and
go into the barn to mow the hay. This is the way we
do in the United States." And that is the way Hassil
Schenck has always done. He recognizes and rec-
ommends the value of honest labor.

Few farmers now living in Indiana have not
heard Schenck's booming and sometimes strident
voice proclaiming the virtues of Farm Bureau
policies and the dangers of not executing them.

Behind such men there are usually good women
to give them reassurance, and sometimes to help
them redefine their plans. President Schenck is most
fortunate in this regard.

Under this Boone County man's leadership, the
stability of the affiliates was undergirded and a sound
relationship established within the family of FB
organizations. As the grain business was Settle's pet
interest, so the growing insurance companies became
a source of pride for President Schenck.

The success of the Indiana organization's development attracted national Farm Bureau attention. As
head of the third, now second, largest membership,
he was a member of the American Farm Bureau
Federation's board of directors for 20 years,—an
elective post. For the last ten years of that tenure
he was a member of the national executive committee.

In 1958 he and the late Senator Harry F. Byrd
of Virginia were honored by the AFBF for distin-

guished and meritorious service to agriculture. For the Indiana leader's contribution to the sale of War Bonds during World War II, he received a framed copy of President Dwight D. Eisenhower's inaugural prayer. He also served on Eisenhower's agricultural advisory committee.

Schenck served, by the Governor's appointment, as trustee of Purdue University for four years. He was a member of the Indiana Sesquicentennial Commission.

The firm leadership of this man, who was made IFB president almost by accident, certainly by no plan of his, became the rock upon which the organization made its greatest growth.

During his long term of office, retiring at 65 years, he traveled extensively going twice to Europe, to South America, Canada, New Zealand, and Australia, besides other shorter distances. He became well versed in the economic life of the nation, but remained conservative in his fiscal philosophy.

In his own community, he has been very generous with his substance, helping in many ways. One of his most rewarding experiences, he recalls, was that of debt conciliator for Boone County farmers whose holdings were threatened during the Depression. Schenck made many friends in that work as he brought mortgagor and mortgagee together to iron out details for satisfactorily paying debts over a longer period than originally agreed upon. This work made it possible for many to hold their farms and pay off their indebtedness. The fact that his work was voluntary won Schenck a firm place of esteem in the community.

+-+

Chapter VII
Firmly Established

+-+

Better Marketing Needed

In the development of any institution or business enterprise, there comes a time when one can say "Now we're in business." The foundations have been laid, principles stated and assimilated into the program, and procedures generally determined. Farmers in Indiana, for the most part, know what to expect of Farm Bureau.

This is not to say there will be no more innovations, or attempts to develop other commercial interests. There will continue to be, it is hoped, a sane business-like approach to problems as they arise.

It can safely be said that Farm Bureau is here to stay. In the original articles of incorporation, the future of the organization was optimistically projected in these words:

"The term, for which this association is to exist, is in perpetuity."

In 1958, farmers began to see the need for developing a strong bargaining organization to represent them in contract negotiations for the sale of their products. They realized that such an organization must be broad enough to include all major producing areas of the product involved, and that a free flow of information from one producing area to another was essential.

To kick off this co-ordinated program, the American Farm Bureau organized the American Agricultural Marketing Association in 1960.

In November, 1961, the Indiana Agricultural

Marketing Association was established as an affiliate of Indiana Farm Bureau. Goals of this program include the improvement of marketing conditions and prices. Through bargaining, producers of any farm crop or livestock can work together to negotiate production contracts with processors and for other improvements in marketing conditions.

While tomato growers were the first to take advantage of the services of the new association, snap bean growers, sweet corn growers and swine producers are beginning to make plans for the future.

Paul T. Norris headed the Association until its management was lodged in the commodity department.

Certain lessons are to be learned from past experience. Charles B. Shuman, president of the American Farm Bureau, warned of the pitfalls in marketing and bargaining when he told representatives from 23 states gathered in Chicago:

"The next year or two is a critical time for the marketing and bargaining program. We must do well what we have to do—make as few mistakes as possible. We must push hard, but not too fast. Now is the time to build sound relations with our producer-members . . . and provide them with accurate information . . . I cannot subscribe to the philosophy that if we sit back and wait, farmers in desperation will join the common cause. A strong, wisely oriented organization is not likely to be built out of weak and desperate members.

These are among the problems that face the members of Indiana's youngest marketing effort. Its success depends on well-informed members and strong local leadership.

First In AFBF

Indiana was one of the 34 states represented at a national meeting called by the American Farm Bureau Federation in early November, 1919, in Chicago. Those states, which had already organized, were asked to go home and propose to their members that they join the Federation.

Indiana proposed that action the very next day in the first annual state convention in Indianapolis to become the first state to do so. Since that time, Hoosier farmers through their organization have been playing a prominent role in the American Farm Bureau.

At first the Indiana Farm Bureau appointed representatives to serve on the board of directors of the national body. In 1924, John Napier Dye and T. I. Ferris were those named from Indiana. At the present time state presidents serve in this capacity and are elected by regions, the number from a region determined by the AFBF by-laws. At the present time the mid-west, of which Indiana is a part, has seven members on the board of 24.

President George Doup was elected to the board upon Schenck's retirement. He was appointed to the executive committee in 1967, and continues in that position. Indiana's consistently large membership has been responsible for maintaing this position of leadership on the national scene; and her leaders have proved equal to the responsibility imposed.

Other honors have come to the Hoosier state in recognition of the effectiveness of its program in information, membership, women's program, commodities, and youth work. Many awards, both symbolic and useful, have been given to those who spearheaded the accomplishments. One has only to walk through the state offices to see evidence of these honors in plaques, flags, and certificates.

To hold high the hand of the AFBF at crucial points in legislative activity in the Congress, Indiana Farm Bureau has many times sent its board of directors to confer with the state's Congressmen. County presidents have gone in groups to register their support or protest of bills vital to farming.

FB and Federal Farm Programs

From the beginning of the Farm Bureau movement in Indiana, farmers have always been aware of the role of the Federal government in agriculture. Sometimes they have been respectful, sometimes suspicious, but always aware.

Their history books had told them of colonial Virginia farmers trying to attain parity in 1621 by limiting tobacco production and burning surpluses. Parity (a fair price, compared to farm costs) has always been the goal. Since the early part of this century, the Federal government has tried to help the nation's farmers reach that goal.

In 1916, the Federal Farm Loan Act, which provided money at reasonable rates of interest and on long-term loans, was welcomed by farmers. They had not been able to get these concessions from local finance sources. This Act set up the Federal Land Banks and the Joint Stock Land Banks. In 1918, the government initiated a program to make direct seed loans.

The first IFB president, John G. Brown, made several trips to Washington, D. C., to seek relief or help from the Federal government. William H. Settle's tenure in the same office was marked with repeated trips to the nation's capital in behalf of some measure which farmers wanted enacted. Presidents since that time have followed suit, though usually now in co-operation with and by joint effort of the American Farm Bureau.

Many current Farm Bureau discussions are about national issues, for it is more and more apparent that agriculture, like other productive businesses, is dependent on world markets. It is also affected by government policies that determine the economic climate. A farmer often may win or lose because of those policies.

In the twenties, the Indiana Farm Bureau leaders worked for the passage of the McNary-Haugen bill, which Congress passed twice only to have it vetoed twice by President Calvin Coolidge. This bill would have established protective tariffs on agricultural products coming into the country. This measure was proposed at a time when our foreign markets had fallen away after World War I, thus causing a sudden and drastic drop in domestic farm prices. The McNary-Haugen bill was in fact retaliatory in nature.

The American Farm Bureau also succeeded in getting an increased appropriation for the Federal Land Banks, which saved thousands of farmers from bankruptcy during the Great Depression. However the simple fact that credit was more readily available did not solve the basic problem of sliding prices and rising costs.

At long last, in 1929, Congress passed the Agricultural Marketing Act, a measure which set up the Federal Farm Board with a half-billion dollar revolving fund. The Board's chief responsibility was to stabilize farm prices.

It attempted to do this by proposing acreage limitations, and it established the farm credit system. The Board also organized a kind of holding corporation, which through its operations was supposed to hold farm commodities off the market until they were needed. The Board also attempted to operate through loans to farm co-operatives. The Indiana

Poultry Co-operative, soon to die, was set up under
this aid. The grain co-ops were also founded under
the Board's aegis.

However, all these efforts were futile, chiefly
because world-wide depression was getting a
stranglehold on the economy. The fact that the
chairman of the board was president of a large farm
implement manufacturing company made some
farmers suspicious of its purposes. The late Sam
Thompson of the Illinois Agricultural Association
(FB) was also a member, however, and can be
supposed to have been adequate protection of farm
interests.

There were those who tried to capitalize on
farmer unrest over the Board's lack of success. The
tenor of the opposition is reflected in a speech made
by the president of the Chicago Board of Trade
before a 1932 convention of National Grain and
Feed Dealers held in French Lick, Indiana. He said:
"I sympathize with the farmers of the nation for
letting the Federal Farm Board and the National
Grain Growers' Corporation bankrupt them."

On the day of the presidential election in November, 1932, Fred Suhre, Bartholomew County FB
leader, and a friend, both Republicans, were dis-
cussing the probable outcome of the voting.

The friend said: "Well, we'll be rid of the Farm
Board." Both tacitly admitted that Franklin D.
Roosevelt would be elected.

Suhre's answer was: "You will get rid of the Farm Board but you will get something you will hate far more."

The farmer's attitude toward government help has been like that of a reluctant bridegroom. He often leans one way and walks another. Older men cannot today forget the relief offices set up for farmers in the twenties. Some of them are a bit reluctant to let go of a "sure thing" though their better judgment leads them in the opposite direction. This divergence of opinion shows up in policy discussions and in delegate sessions, but the "sure-thingers" are growing fewer and fewer as they better understand the principles of the market price system.

By and large, Indiana Farm Bureau members have demonstrated courage and good judgment in the policies they have developed. There have been faltering moments, as back in 1925 when state taxes had increased 312 per cent in two years, the public debt by 400 per cent, and farm leaders through the pages of The HOOSIER FARMER asked that the Federal government initiate measures to cause inflation and thus raise farm prices. They fallaciously thought perhaps that inflation would raise farm prices without raising farm costs. It could have for short periods of time, but not in the long run.

The National Co-operative Marketing Act, permissive in nature, was passed in 1926, a year after the Indiana General Assembly had passed a bill permitting co-ops to function,—this Act largely on the instigation of I. H. Hull. Today the national statute has been extended in application to include a program of research, education, advisory assistance, and financial aid for co-ops.

The Agricultural Extension Act in 1914 was very slow in getting into full application, and then only through the persistent and material support of farmers. In Indiana, it was Farm Bureau which reached out and helped the Extension Service to its feet. This Service is one effort of the Federal government that has been wholly acceptable to farm people.

As the Government stepped in to aid farmers toward a better standard of living, some industry leaders and businessmen began to show resentment against this expenditure of tax money. Yet we must not forget that the Reconstruction Finance Corporation was established to help business in distress; and even today there is a similar source of financial aid for small businesses.

Perhaps not fully realizing what they were asking for, Indiana Farm Bureau worked diligently for the passage of the first Agricultural Adjustment Act, passed in 1933. They had been convinced that the withholding action which took place under the Federal Farm Board was not equal to the problem. All Indiana Congressmen voted unanimously for what became known as the Triple A. While the Federal Farm Board had worked through co-ops, the AAA went around co-ops and made contracts directly with farmers.

In a contract the farmer agreed to reduce acreage and hog numbers. The first loans on corn were made in October, 1933, at 45 cents per bushel. This was the era when a farmer agreed to kill his surplus pigs. Chauncey Downey, who last spring (1967) planted his sixty-ninth corn crop on his Morgan County farm, recalls some of the details of the hectic Triple A days. Pigs under 70 pounds were sorted out for slaughtering or "plowing under" as some called the process of cut-back. Those under 70 pounds were marked with a red crayon and those over 70, with a green one. In other words, the green-marked ones got the "grow light."

But the public, that often insensitive body of nameless citizens, rose with one accord to scream about the brutality of the program. The idea of killing pigs shocked them. Yet they continued to buy and eat pork from larger hogs. Somehow the idea of killing pigs offended their sense of morality, and the act took on the aspects of man's inhumanity to pigs.

The Triple A marked the beginning of an era during which the Federal government has broadened its program far beyond the original assignment in research and regulation. In 1933 the USDA had 26,544 employees. By 1937, there were 106,217, of which 93,797 worked outside the District of Columbia. This huge staff was made necessary by the provisions and enforcement of the AAA. By 1961, this number had been reduced by some

20,000. By November 30, 1967, there were reportedly 113,185 on the USDA payroll.

The '33 Act provided production controls on wheat, cotton, rice, tobacco, corn, hogs, and dairy products with benefits paid to co-operating producers. These payments were made from taxes levied on food processors. The production control features and the processor tax were found unconstitutional by the U.S. Supreme Court in 1936.

When the USDA left out farm organizations in this try at solving farm problems, and worked directly with farmers in obtaining contracts under the Triple A, FB membership interest froze. One charter member today claims that the omnipresent arm of Government around the farmer's shoulders can be blamed for a lack of interest in his local Farm Bureau. At first blush, it seems much easier to let someone else solve our problems for us.

Figures reflect the fact that the IFB membership during the thirties stood almost still. Farmers, and often their wives, liked the jobs given them by the local Triple A Agency on the county committees.

Later in the year 1936, after the Court had outlawed the Act, the Soil Conservation and Domestic Allotment Act made a feeble attempt to control production. Sixty-two per cent of the farmers of the nation had signed contracts under the AAA.

A second Agricultural Adjustment Act passed in 1938 that provided for cross-compliance, tying quotas to acreage allotments. It originally provided for mandatory price supports on corn, wheat, and cotton, with permissive supports for other commodities. It also strengthened the conservation features of the Domestic Allotment Act and provided crop insurance.

The Commodity Credit Corporation, which was established under the President's emergency powers in 1933, has since then supported prices on more than 100 different commodities, through the permissive clause of the AAA.

According to Claude Wickard, the Ever Normal Granary idea, credited to governmental leaders, came from the mind of Earl Smith, Illinois farmer who became president of the Illinois (FB) Agricultural Association and vice-president of the AFBF. This idea of stockpiling food, much as shipping facilities are subsidized and minerals stockpiled for cases of emergency by the U.S., made the aid to farmers through storage a bit more acceptable to the public. USDA Secretary Henry A. Wallace turned to King Pharaoh in the Bible story for authority to recommend the wisdom of storing grain. It would work to the advantage of both the consumer and producer, it was argued.

Let us remember that most of the features that went into the early farm programs were suggested by organized farmers, and many of those early efforts that proved futile have remained to haunt farm leaders today. They must now find a better way. At first high, protective tariffs, then export subsidies and price supports—all were tried, but all were interferences in the normal procedures of the market system, and all failed.

While there have been numerous amendments to the 1938 AAA, it remains in its basic form as the legislation undergirding most farm program law today.

During the 1950's and early 60's, high government price supports caused mounting surpluses of some farm commodities, but political leaders were afraid to let go of the "carrot." To reduce surpluses, administrative leaders tried to win farmer approval of an elaborate compensatory payment and limited land retirement program for wheat, but farmers by referendum said "No." Within a year, Congress enacted the very program that farmers had rejected by more than a 2 to 1 majority.

From 1964 until 1967, government surpluses of grain had dropped drastically due to foreign demand and increased domestic use. In the same period, farm prices for wheat and feed grains had fallen to new 30-year lows, attributable largely to the government's compensatory payment programs which price them out of the export market when faced with competition from other countries.

FB Program Today

Through the years of trial and error and experience, Farm Bureau has developed a program which it feels will revive net farm income by controlling production and returning to the law of supply and demand. The plan couples a program of government-backed recourse commodity loans to farmers with an enlarged land retirement program.

It is felt that, if implemented, the program will allow farmers to make their own management decisions, keep large surplus grain stocks out of the hands of government, relieve the farmer of the necessity of selling his grain at harvest time when the prices may be lowest, and will encourage farmers to hold unneeded land out of production until needed for added food production.

To those who occasionally ask "What has happened to Farm Bureau?" in referring to its present conservative stand on most issues, this statement by an early leader in a 1923 HOOSIER FARMER is revealing:

"By an autocratic system of governmental price fixing, the minimum price would become the maximum price; the producer would, in effect, become a ward of the government. The very democracy of the Republic would be imperiled." This was said before they had crop-control legislation.

American Farm Bureau President Charles B. Shuman said in a Lansing, Michigan, address in June, 1963: "Farm Bureau decided we were going in the wrong direction about 16 years ago. The wheat referendum (May, 1963) made it (the decision) emphatic." He said this after farmers had crop control legislation on a national scale.

In scanning old records and the pro and con discussions on issues that confronted the organization, one can easily discern that there has always been a representation of the less conservative members active in the IFB, but they have been in the minority. That they have been encouraged to speak out on their differences of opinion is a credit to the organization, and a contribution to its vigor.

In the development of national farm legislation Farm Bureau has from its inception been very active, however not always able to implement its policies. And while this vast network of laws and regulations were being written into the books, a staff and budget to make them function were acquired. And once the budgetary camel got his nose into the tent, he gave every promise of becoming the major occupant. In 1961, the total agricultural net income of the nation stood at $12.8 billion, while the U.S. Department of Agriculture budget was nearly $7.3 billion. In all fairness, it must be pointed out that some of the budget is spent for maintenance of national forests enjoyed by all citizens. There are other such expenditures not wholly in the interest of agriculture.

A comprehensive, governmental farm credit system has developed simultaneously with Farm Bureau. Since their founding, some of these financial endeavors have become wholly farmer-owned, and some have remained governmental. For those who may be concerned about the government threat to private banking or credit resources, these figures may be revealing:

In 1966 individuals and merchants held 41 per cent of the debts owed by farmers; banks, 26.4 per cent; insurance companies, 12 per cent; Farm Credit Administration, 17.3 per cent; and the Farmers Home Administration (government credit agency), 3.3 per cent.

Progressive Conservatism

The program of the Indiana Farm Bureau has always been far-reaching. From the first, it went on record for the improvement of rural schools, the invigoration of rural churches, for raising the standard of farm living, and for farm youth guidance. From the first, it has been in the avant-garde for good citizenship.

Born on the eve of the final Victory Loan drive in World War I, the organization announced this pledge:

"The new Federation pledges its hearty support, declaring that it has no other tasks before it and no other responsibilities until it has done its full share in this Victory Loan campaign."

Contrary to popular opinion, farmers long ago broke the bonds of isolationism in their own thinking. A New York dateline newspaper article during President Woodrow Wilson's administration made this statement: "An overwhelming majority of the 12 million farmers of America favor the entrance

of the United States into the League of Nations,—"
an espousal due for disappointment when it was
defeated by Congress.

Farm Bureau has given its moral support to the
United Nations since its founding in 1945.

In the first IFB convention in 1919, Indiana
farmers let it be known they were not to be confused
with radicals. A resolution was passed asking that:
"We express our faith in Almighty God, and our
unlimited confidence in the patriotism of our fellow
farmers . . . that we absolutely condemn I.W.W.-ism,
Bolshevism, anarchy, or any other form of such
madness in whatever form it may appear; and no
person advocating any such ism can be a member
of this organization."

This bit of background philosophy indicates the
nature of the program that springs from it and the
character of the people who make up its constituency.

The program itself has always been concerned
with marketing, transportation, education, taxes, and
economics. In the April, 1920, issue of The
HOOSIER FARMER an editorial lauded a conference of 1,500 clergymen from 20 denominations,
come together to attempt to unite the Christian
churches. The women's department conducts a continuing program of encouragement through awards
to country churches that have improved their
facilities and programs.

The first state convention passed a resolution
asking for better schools. On June 7, 1920, the

board of directors asked of the state's school authorities that vocational instructors be placed in each township for full-time service. The 1934 convention recommended that rural teacher training laboratories be established under the supervision of the state Board of Education and be administered by state teacher training institutions. The Indiana Farm Bureau in 1963 was influential in getting a state law passed to provide for the establishment of a new type of vocational education.

Called the Indiana Vocational Technical College, it is post high school and non-academic in its curriculum, which is designed wholly to train men and women for jobs that call for special skills. The fast pace at which industry has become automated has left many workers jobless. To solve this problem of unemployment and at the same time provide industry with trained workers is the goal of this unique venture in education. While there may be several specific centers established for this instruction, it may be found more practical and more attractive to contract with local public school administrators or with colleges and universities to use their facilities and some of their faculty in their leisure time. Contracts may also be made with industry for the use of its facilities.

The plan is unique. Other states are inquiring about the Indiana venture into this new field of education. Soon, there may be such vocational or technical instruction in every county.

The new College has consideration in the state's program of support, along with Purdue, Indiana University, Ball State University, and Indiana State University.

Indiana Farm Bureau can take particular pride in this development, since Vice-President Glenn W. Sample has been active in it from the first and has now the office of chairman of the board of trustees. Representatives on this group of seven include one each from labor, manufacturing, business or professions, agriculture, two at large, one of whom must be a woman, and the State Superintendent of Public Instruction, all appointed by the Governor, except the Superintendent.

Farmers will directly benefit from this kind of education. Some of their sons who find it desirable to leave farming may now receive training for other job opportunity.

One could rightly say that those vocational instructors in each township, asked by the 1920 delegate body, may yet materialize.

Another significant move made in 1920, to study the possibility of a Great Lakes-to-Ocean Waterway now finds this waterway developed. The Indiana Farm Bureau is presently concerned with the building of a port to make use of this water route.

The organization department of the IFB has grown from a one-man staff to 23 at the present. Larry Brandon as its director was the first to employ fieldmen, who were George R. Harvey and Hubert Ellison, both of whom were farm reared school teachers. The director today is Hollys E. Moon. Working with him are 20 fieldmen (two per district), one assistant director, and one specially assigned to local affairs work.

This department obviously must depend a great deal on local leaders and lay members in soliciting members; but the fact that each year more than 85 per cent or better than 75,000 send their dues by mail without personal contact having been made is evidence of the confidence these farmers have in their organization.

These employees are imbued with FB philosophy and constitute a work force much more effective than the part-time solicitors hired in earlier days.

The local affairs program, spearheaded by the organization department but implemented at the local level, has made significant contributions to good government. Under this plan, Farm Bureau committees of men interested in good government serve as watchdogs, call on county officials, inquire into spending programs, and represent farmer interest in what is going on.

The information department was one of the first set up in the state organization. While there is no way to measure effectiveness, we are told that while L. L. Needler was state secretary, he had 400 local

reporters feeding information to the state office.
Mailing printed information to members has saved
many miles of driving in order to contact members.
In the early years the information department was
primarily devoted to publishing The HOOSIER
FARMER. Its work has grown much beyond that
today to include news releases, public relations programs and materials, posters and booklets for county
fair displays, and other such promotional pieces.
Radio and television over the years have also been
used to advantage. Edmond Foust, one-time editor
of The HOOSIER FARMER also personally conducted a radio program for a time. Magnetic tape is
now prepared in advance in many instances. By this
almost constant flow of information, farmers become
better equipped to make sound judgments in the
formation of organizational policy.

The information department is also responsible
for giving guidance in a public relations for agriculture program in all parts of this state. While this
is not new, it was given new impetus about 15 years
ago.

In 1923 the Lebanon Rotarians and Kiwanians
invited county Farm Bureau officials to lunch prior
to the launching of the Bureau's annual membership
drive. This kind of encouragement existed in many
small town communities. As early as 1920 Rush
county businessmen closed their stores and shops
while they honored the farmers of the area. Five
thousand are reported to have been present. In

Bluffton, 60 businessmen donned aprons and served dinner to Wells county farmers. Shelbyville and Vincennes had similar events.

Today, exchange visits and discussions of their mutual or diverse problems occur in the form of luncheons or dinners, tours of each other's facilities, or exchange visits in homes. A few years ago, a high school class of New York private school students came to spend a week on Indiana farms. The next fall they invited the young people from the host farms to New York to visit them in their homes. This was a most revealing and educational experience for both groups.

Editors of the magazine and heads of the information department over the years have been, in order of their service: Dr. C. W. Hickman, Lewis Taylor, E. E. Reynolds, Perry Crane, William Stahl, James Moore, Edmond Foust, Glenn W. Sample, and the incumbent, C. W. Stall. Except for the years 1926 through 1931, when it was published semi-monthly, the magazine has been issued monthly.

The education department (established in early '36) so-called because of its prime purpose of channeling information to farm youth, was started by M. K. Derrick, to be followed as director by C. L. Dyer, Warren O'Hara, and now by Estel Callahan. The department is responsible for all youth programs sponsored by Farm Bureau. This includes the Indiana Rural Youth, co-sponsored by Purdue

University Co-operative Extension Service; Future
Farmers of America; Future Homemakers of
America; 4-H Clubs; and others.

The Rural Youth program occupies perhaps more
time than any other group. Designed for youth from
18 till 30 years old, this program encourages education and participation in local government, study of
current issues, planned recreation, and community
service. There are now between three and four
thousand members, many of whom work in town.

The education department is supported not only
by the parent organization but also by the Indiana
Farm Bureau Co-operative Association, FB insurance companies, Mid-West Creameries, Inc., and
the Pure Milk Association. In return for this financial
aid, the program under the guidance of the department staff of four helps promote dairy month activities, participates in schools of instruction on the
co-operative philosophy and function, and in FB
information.

In recent years, some education staff member has
acted as instructor at an annual Economic Workshop
held at Lake Oliver in northeastern Indiana for
teachers of high school pupils and for clergymen.
This effort has been undertaken by labor, agriculture,
and industry because leaders felt that teachers are
in a strategic position to teach sound economics,
and that clergymen are especially needed in the
defense of free enterprise.

Supporting organizations of the Workshop pay the expenses of the enrollees. Many schools, as a result, have incorporated into their curricula the principles of economics even at first grade level. The FB family contributes $3,500 annually to this program.

For several years, education department staff members have taken leadership in an Indiana Youthpower Conference attended by state leaders of some 10 youth clubs and organizations in the state. At this two-day conference the 200 young leaders take part in an intensive program designed to emphasize the importance of food and nutrition to vibrant health and a strong nation. Cooperating in this statewide program are many organizations and businesses interested in the food business.

In the field of public education, IFB members have always been cognizant of the needs of their public schools. In the difficult years from 1930-33, according to Guy Cantwell, who was working in the field of education at the time, 18 southern Indiana counties were supplying 50 per cent of the teachers for northern Indiana. This fact pointed up the great need for spreading educational costs on a per-pupil basis, as state aid is now based. Southern counties were admittedly not as wealthy, yet their youth went on to institutions of higher learning and so needed good elementary and secondary training to prepare them.

In later years, the question of school consolidation and reorganization has often kept a local FB meet-

ing overtime while the heated arguments ran on.
The state organization, by adopted policies, has not
taken a stand on this issue, because the factors
involved vary by community. It has encouraged
instead the active local participation of farmers in
whatever decision is made, so that their interests will
be protected.

The commodity department, with a staff of five,
replaced the livestock department. Marion Stack-
house as director is supported in the program by
county and district advisory commodity committees.
There are committees on livestock, poultry, dairy,
field crops, and fruits and vegetables. County committees discuss their problems, make recommendations to the district groups, who in turn suggest
action to the Indiana Farm Bureau board of directors. This body submits the recommendations to the
state resolutions committee and finally to the delegate
body.

The commodity staff also participates in quality
improvement programs, and in carrying education
to farmers about new possibilities in their particular
fields of production. Farm Bureau's new farm
record keeping service is operated by this department,
and marketing improvement programs are under
continuous consideration.

Farm Bureau has from the first been interested
in foreign trade. Today the production from one
acre in six moves out in export. This rate is subject

to national policies, however, and so trade becomes involved in national politics.

The isolated self-sufficient farmer of former times had only a limited access to products of the world . . . oranges at Christmas and gunpowder at exorbitant prices. Trade with other parts of the world and better transportation within our own country have changed all this. Every conceivable food now appears on the farmer's local grocery or supermarket shelves—five or six thousand items, in fact.

The tax and legislative department, now headed by Vance L. Denney, has always been involved in some tax issue when the General Assembly opens biennially. Property taxes have been a source of constant irritation among farmers, and dozens of other issues affecting farmers require the attention of FB lobbyists.

Once the elected delegates decide what action they want taken at the state level, staff members begin to lay their plans for the introduction of bills needed. Farm Bureau lobbyists must first find sympathetic support. Advance studies by official committees or by lay groups can do much to prepare the way for acceptance of a proposed bill.

Leaders have also found over the years that a bill stands a better chance of passage if it has support from both parties. The organization's record of success speaks for the merit of its proposals.

For a number of years, IFB maintained a research department to compile and file for reference pertinent facts pertaining to agriculture and to matters of interest to farmers. This resource has been of help to state leaders.

Larry Wright of the state staff works with the local FB and insurance company offices in coordinating their paper work, so that through uniformity of records, efficiency may be established.

Increasing tempo in the area of natural resources development led to the establishment by Indiana Farm Bureau in 1966 of a natural resources department. The department is headed by Acord Cantwell. Its program consists chiefly of working with local FB leaders in development of organization policy in the natural resources field, advising local FB groups on natural resources problems, and representing FB in state and national meetings of farm leaders considering natural resources.

Late in 1962, the Indiana Farm Bureau established the Farm Bureau Foundation, through which endowments, contributions, bequests, and other funds may be made available to qualified students through loans and grants. Since that time, it had as of late '67 made grants of $12,000 and loans totaling $6,150. Interest rates are made attractive. The Modlin Memorial Fund, established in 1929 upon the sudden death of a women's department head, Mrs. Harry Modlin of New Castle, was merged into the Foundation fund. FB grants are also replenished by pennies and nickels given at local FB meetings to be given to ten Purdue Agricultural Short Course students and to ten young women enrolled in institutions of post high school learning.

Attempts have been made to measure the actual material support given to farm youth at all levels of the organization. Though only a rough estimate has been arrived at, it is believed, from spot summaries made, that to 4-H work alone, Farm Bureau people donate between $50,000 and $70,000 annually. In addition, the Indiana Farm Bureau Co-operative Association has a year round program for Future Farmers. State FFA officers are brought to Indianapolis each year by the IFBCA and FB for brief education in the organizations' philosophies and procedures. They also conduct an annual school for Rural Youth, usually with about 100 attending.

Besides the monetary help given these youth groups, Farm Bureau people, both leaders and lay members, contribute a great deal of time as adult leaders. They buy club pins, pay expenses of earned trips, and give achievement dinners for 4-H club members of the community.

Thus is the future of farm leadership given some assurance of rising to its responsibilities with good training.

President George Doup, who heads Indiana's largest, general farm organization, is the product of a "century farm" which, in reality more than a hundred years ago was transferred by grant from the Government to his forebears. He still resides on that land near Columbus in Bartholomew county, where he and his brother, Perry, have a joint enterprise.

From early manhood, George's common-sense judgment and other leadership qualities won him the respect of other young people in the community and of Farm Bureau leaders like Maurice Douglas, then district FB director, and Fred Suhre.

As a young man, George worked for the formation of the Indiana Rural Youth Club, and was elected its first president.

As an employee of the Farmers Marketing Association (FB affiliated) in Bartholomew county, under the wise tutelage of Manager Suhre, George continued to grow in stature and experience. He was elected the eighth FB district director in 1945, following Douglas, and resigned this position in 1951 to join the state staff as livestock director.

Upon the resignation of Vice-President Larry Brandon in 1952 in mid-term, George was appointed to fill out his term. The next biennial election by the delegate body continued him in that office, where he served until 1957.

With his experience and success as a youth leader, FB director, FB employee, and FB vice-president, it is little wonder that the delegates selected him to head the organization when Hassil E. Schenck retired. Doup has been re-elected five times since becoming president in 1958.

In addition to his state duties, he has had many civic and national assignments. He has been a member of the American Farm Bureau Board of Directors since '58 and has served on the executive committee since '67. In the spring of '63, he was sent by the AFBF as its representative in the role of observer at the conference of the International Federation of Agricultural Producers, held in Bray, Ireland. In 1967, as a member of an American Farm Bureau team he visited Lima, Peru, to confer with farm organization officials of eight South American countries on agricultural trade between South America and the U. S.

In studying the qualities of the five presidents, it is readily seen that no one has tried to ape his predecessor. Doup embodies characteristics quite opposite to those possessed by Schenck. He is quiet, deliberate and unassuming. He is very careful to choose the right word for the occasion. He employs a business-like approach to problems, and exercises a great deal of suavity to gain his ends.

President Doup can be firm, however, if the occasion demands it. He is a family man and is active in the Presbyterian Church.

Age of Rapid Change

In this era of our national development, change is rampant. Today's invention is tomorrow's obsolescence. What is this doing to agriculture and to the farm organization, for it cannot be a thing apart?

The solidarity of the membership is reaffirmed annually in the voluntary enrollment and payment of dues. There are those who cry: "Why don't the farm organizations get together?" Farm Bureau leaders must always answer: "We cannot forsake or compromise policies drawn up by duly elected delegates, just for the sake of presenting a united front in agriculture." Too, Farm Bureau represents more farmers than all other general farm organizations combined. Why dilute its strength of conviction and numbers?

There have been a few attempts to organize farmers into trade unions. J. Walter Thompson, former fifth district director, recalled one such incident that happened many years ago when the United Mine Workers, Local Number 50, called a meeting in Parke county to try to organize dairy formers. The inducement offered was a guarantee of higher prices. Thompson credits the failure of the meeting partially to the fact that the union leader who addressed them was unusually obese, and when he talked his stomach quivered like a bowl full of jelly."

It was so disconcerting that "I couldn't keep my

mind on what he was saying," he related. Not a single membership card was signed.

Other such overtures have been made in other parts of the state, but without success. Farmers have traditionally frowned upon trade union tactics. Early pronouncements of principle made this unmistakably clear. They repeatedly through the years have said: "No strikes, no violence,—and no isms."

They were on guard against a rash of isms in the world, pointed up by communism's promises, later discredited as empty and dangerous. A quotation from the editor's page of a 1936 HOOSIER FARMER indicated that farmers were keeping abreast of world developments:

"There is practically no farm tenancy in Denmark. Co-operation has resulted in the recovery of farm ownership . . . which demonstrates that communism is not necessary to eliminate tenancy." Co-operation in farmers' commercial ventures has proved, in fact, to be a buffer against both extremes of the economic pendulum.

While trade unions had achieved greater material benefits for their members, farmers did not approve of methods used. They proposed to solve their own problems, and still do, by united action through business principles.

There have been many significant changes on the farm. In 1919 there were 218,000 farms of five acres or more in Indiana. Today there are about

108,000, or a little less than half as many. Today the investment per farm worker on Indiana's average commercial farm is more than $100,000 compared to $17,500 per industrial worker.

What has happened to Farm Bureau membership in the meantime? At the beginning of the second year of the organization's existence, 973 townships were organized out of a total of 1,016. In 1920 the paid membership was 64,420. Today there are about 850 local Farm Bureaus and membership in the state is more than 153,000.

In the early days virtually all members were farmers, but as farm numbers have diminished and membership has grown, it becames obvious that some of today's members are non-farm people. Increasing interest of people, in various agribusiness organizations and industries, in farm policy and other programs in which FB was active has led to Farm Bureau's providing in 1948 for a non-voting, Associate, classification of membership for people who are not farmers. Most who join in this category are interested in lending their support to FB programs and policies or join to get other services offered by the organization to its members.

In the beginning, the annual enrollment of members was done in a burst of enthusiasm when economic conditions were favorable. When times were hard, membership dropped in direct proportion to the severity of the times.

Some of the enthusiasm is reflected in an account

of the first convention of the IFB. Benton county had won the silver cup for being first "over the top" —a war-spawned expression. It had reached its $200 fund quota set by state officers to help the treasury. Bartholomew county was second, and when its president W. H. Newson received a flag as an award, someone shouted "Let's sing." There followed a stanza of My Country, 'Tis of Thee.

The first applications for membership in the state Federation came from Bartholomew, Benton, Gibson, Hancock, Harrison, Henry, Jackson, Jefferson, Lake, Madison, Marion, Orange, Parke, Pulaski, Ripley, Spencer, Tippecanoe, Vanderburgh, Vigo, and Warren counties—with Henry claiming to be first within the fold.

Many townships still hold 11 monthly meetings and join with others in the county for an annual picnic or fall meeting. Some have turned to joint meetings to get a larger turn-out. Television is sometimes the winner over the local FB meeting.

One county decided to join forces with the 'picture box.' Leaders had inadvertently set a meeting date on a night when a popular prize fight was scheduled. When they discovered their competion, they installed a TV set in the meeting place, conducted the program until fight time, stopped long enough to watch it, then returned to the business at hand. Attendance was very good that night.

Other and more competitive influences have arisen outside the organization. For example, about one-

third of the farmers in the state work part-time
away from home. This is especially true near large
cities and of small farmers. George W. Elliott of
Rising Sun reports that from 5 till 7:30 a.m. the
stream of cars past his house carrying farm people
to Cincinnati to work is almost bumper-to-bumper.
Many wives also work away from home.

The question is occasionally asked, where will
their allegiance be, to agriculture or to their labor
union? Farmers are becoming either two-job workers
or large farm operators. In either case, they can
justifiably argue they do not have time to be county
or local FB president.

There was a threat to the farm co-ops in the trend
toward larger farms until co-ops decided to keep in
step. Marvin Briggs, in an address before the
American Institute of Co-operation in August, 1963,
at Lincoln, Nebraska, hinted at this:

"His (the farmer's) purchases will move from
factory (directly) to farm to cut unnecessary costs;
and many of his sales will move directly to the processor to eliminate duplication" (of handling).

There is much more at stake than finding someone
to be president of the local organization. Those who
work in agriculture have always been considered a
bulwark of personal liberty and independence,
though both qualities have been somewhat diminished in the last quarter century. To preserve the
right to manage his own farm, yet have a fair return
for his efforts, is the number one problem facing

the farmer today,—even as it was in 1919, yet with greater urgency on the modern scene.

Some ground has been given and some gains made. The American Farm Bureau Federation enjoys the reputation of standing four-square to preserve farmers' freedom. But it needs the active support of the 1.7 million members back home. A leader gives guidance. Members must give strength and rootedness to the leader.

J. Edgar Scholl, of Fayette county, has some biting words to say about the over-zealous who want to seek government help at every turn:

"Our country was built on a system of free enterprise and should not embrace socialism. To hark back to inequities that may have existed many years ago should not be used as an excuse for present day unethical standards. Whether we approve or not, great changes have come in all aspects of life and our challenge is to meet them."

So any modern citizen like today's FB member has a most difficult assignment,—that of becoming integrated into community life and yet remaining an individual with a mind of his own.

The free enterprise system is based on the necessity and ability to test oneself against others. The Greeks call it agon—wrestling for excellence, within oneself as well as with outside forces. Farm Bureau is the instrument by which and through which the individual farmer can wrestle with and succeed against these forces,—if he gives the best he has.

Anson Thomas reminds us that we "will never accomplish all the members and leaders hope for, because ours is a give and take society."

It is imperative that every member, every leader, every policy be directed toward exerting the greatest possible influence for good on public life and on agriculture. The organization is a seedbed of leadership and the furrow which leads toward a sound agriculture. But as Albert Ferris says:

"We carry this treasure in earthen vessels. In Farm Bureau, we should marshal our forces of combined opinion behind legislation and education needed to bring production in line with demand . . . As long as we keep a nice balance between intelligent conservatism and enlightened progressiveness, we should continue to meet our obligations."

John Curry of Sullivan county, another member concerned about maintaining organizational vigor, says: "I can only hope that as we oldtimers leave the scene, our younger generation will see fit to carry on with vigor and enlightenment, and improve the opportunities for united action. United action—that is the key."

One thing is sure. Farmers cannot take Farm Bureau for granted. A net worth of more than $2 million cannot make it live and function as it was designed to do, unless the members make it happen.

The Indiana Farm Bureau needs many leaders, who, in the words of Josiah Gilbert Holland, written a century ago, are:

State FB headquarters (at left) is on the 11th floor in the newly remodeled FB Insurance Building, 130 E. Washington St., Indianapolis.

Cradle of IFB was the old English Hotel on Monument Circle, Indianapolis, where the organizational meeting for the Indiana Federation of Farmers' Associations took place in March 1919.

Tomlinson Hall, Indianapolis, was the scene of early state FB conventions until 1942.

(Above): Farm Bureau's legislative team (Hollys Moon and Vance L. Denney, second and third from left) visit with senators and other lobbyists outside the State Senate in the Statehouse.

Farm Bureau at The Legislature

(At Right): FB members, 15,000 strong, march to the Statehouse on February 23, 1939 to save the Gross Income Tax from repeal.

(Below): More than 10,000 gathered at the Statehouse on February 16, 1933 to urge passage of the Ind. Gross Income Tax Law. Circled is FB President Settle who led the march.

Grain Handling

Modern railroad car "dump" at I.F.B.C.A. Indianapolis elevator is typical of today's modern Co-op grain-handling equipment in service for efficient marketing.

(Below): Hoosier farmers thresh with Co-op threshing machine. The year 1935.

Farm Bureau
Is The Big Voice
Of Indiana Agriculture

"Tall men, sun-crowned, who live above the fog
In public duty and in private thinking."

Conceived in hope, born in travail, nurtured in trial and error, and maturing with pride. That is Farm Bureau. A great body of human endeavor has gone into its development, which will not end so long as the program shifts to meet the needs of the people on the land.

In his final message to the state convention in 1957, retiring IFB president Hassil E. Schenck, put it another way:

"We are at the point in our organized efforts when we will not meet defeat from the outside. If we meet defeat, it will be through the farmers' own action. If there is a deterioration of the organization, it will be from the forces within. It is your job as members of Farm Bureau and/or agricultural cooperative endeavors, to see to it that your hired men—your officers, directors, staff members and employees in all these endeavors shall work constructively together to serve your best interests.

Your organization and your cooperatives are your servants, not your master. You run them; never allow them to run you!"

Addenda

INDIANA FARM BUREAU OFFICERS

1919

President, John G. Brown, White County; first vice-president, W. H. Hickman, Blackford County; second vice-president, E. E. Reynolds, Tippecanoe County; general secretary, Lewis Taylor, Warrick County; treasurer, Charles G. Chester, Lake County.

1920

President, John G. Brown; first-president, Everett McClure, Dearborn County; second vice-president, Maurice Douglas, Shelby County; general secretary, Lewis Taylor; treasurer, E. E. Reynolds; recording secretary, Perry Crane, Boone County.

1921

President, John G. Brown; first vice-president, Maurice Douglas; second vice-president, Everett McClure; treasurer, E. E. Reynolds; general secretary, Perry Crane.

1922

President, John G. Brown; first vice-president, Everett McClure; second vice-president, Scott Meiks, Shelby County; treasurer, Lewis Taylor; general secretary, Perry Crane.

1923

President, William H. Settle, Wells County; first vice-president, Scott Meiks; second vice-president, Ray L. Bradley, Montgomery County; treasurer, Lewis Taylor; general secretary, Perry Crane.

1924

President, William H. Settle; first vice-president, Scott Meiks; second vice-president, James G. Covert, Johnson County; treasurer, Lewis Taylor; general secretary, Perry Crane.

1925

President, William H. Settle; first vice-president, Scott Meiks; second vice-president, Mrs. Charles W. Sewell, Benton County; treasurer, Lewis Taylor; general secretary, Perry Crane.

1926

President, William H. Settle; first vice-president, Lewis Taylor; second vice-president, Mrs. Charles W. Sewell; secretary-treasurer, Perry Crane.

1927-1934

President, William H. Settle; first vice-president, Lewis Taylor; second vice-president, Mrs.

Charles W. Sewell; secretary-treasurer, L. L. Needler, Grant County.

1935

President, Lewis Taylor; first vice-president, Hassil E. Schenck, Boone County; second vice-president through January, Mrs. Charles W. Sewell (at that time Mrs. Sewell was chosen to be administrative director of the Associated Women of AFBF); Mrs. Benjamin Scott, Hendricks County, was chosen second vice-president and began her service in April; A. S. Thomas, Hendricks County, served as secretary of the organization during the months of February and March, succeeding Mrs. Fenton. In April the duties of acting secretary and treasurer became the responsibility of Vice-President Schenck, and L. L. Needler served as director of organization.

1936

President, Lewis Taylor; first vice-president and acting secretary-treasurer, Hassil E. Schenck; second vice-president, Mrs. Benjamin Scott, Hendricks County.

1937-1946

Mr. Taylor was re-elected to a two-year term as president in November, 1936, but died in

December of that year. Vice-president, Hassil
E. Schenck, Boone County, was named acting
president by the board of directors, and was
subsequently elected to the presidency. Larry
B. Brandon, DeKalb County, was appointed,
then elected to fill the vice-presidency; second
vice-president, Mrs. Benjamin Scott.

1947 1951

President, Hassil E. Schenck; first vice-president and secretary-treasurer, Larry Brandon;
second vice-president, Mrs. Russell Cushman,
Hancock County.

1952-1954

President, Hassil E. Schenck; vice-president
and secretary-treasurer, Larry Brandon (until
his resignation in July, 1952); then George
Doup, Bartholomew County, was appointed,
later elected to the vice-president and secretary-treasurer's position; second vice-president, Mrs. Russell Cushman.

1955-1957

President, Hassil E. Schenck; vice-president
and secretary-treasurer, George Doup; second
vice-president, Mrs. Paul Flinn, Johnson
County; when she became too ill to fill the
position, Mrs. Guy E. Gross, Whitley County,

was appointed by the board of directors to fill the remaining year and a half of Mrs. Flinn's term.

1958

President, George Doup, first vice-president and secretary-treasurer, Glenn W. Sample, Boone County; second vice-president, Mrs. Guy Gross; the duties of secretary-treasurer (nonelective) were assigned to George R. Harvey, Marion County, in November, 1958.

1959-1968

President, George Doup; vice-president, Glenn W. Sample; second vice-president, Mrs. Guy E. Gross; secretary-treasurer, George R. Harvey.

MEMBERSHIP RECORD

W hile figures are not available on the exact number of members in the Indiana Farm Bureau at the end of the first year; it is known that all 92 counties had organized; 973 townships of a possible 1,016 had organized. By the end of the second year, 1921, membership stood at 64,420 — a figure not to be attained again until 1946.

This slide reflected the lack of cash, the failure of the new co-operatives to deliver on what the farmers expected of them, and the internal struggle that was taking place in bringing order out of chaos. This diversion of interest and energy did not allow time for soliciting members.

The membership figures for all these years reflect these forces:

1922-39,973	1938-26,009	1953-108,882
1923-42,489	1939-25,858	1954-116,907
1924-40,874	1940-27,869	1955-124,025
1925-35,511	1941-30,528	1956-130,163
1926-38,181	1942-35,032	1957-133,219
1927-35,520	1943-44,448	1958-130,703
1928-36,017	1944-49,795	1959-130,896
1929-31,353	1945-58,262	1960-129,479
1930-33,450	1946-70,885	1961-127,888
1931-33,055	1947-85,435	1962-129,342
1932-25,167	1948-92,779	1963-131,476
1933-23,587	1949-86,173	1964-135,898
1934-26,327	1950-90,912	1965-140,354
1935-27,570	1951-96,621	1966-148,760
1936-26,521	1952-101,561	1967-153,162
1937-28,991		1968-158,400+

DISTRICT DIRECTORS

1919

1-J. A. Warren, Porter County; 2-Hugh M. Widney, DeKalb; 3-C. W. Hickman, Tippecanoe; 4-H. T. Walker, Blackford; 5-W. F. Franklin, Hendricks, and Oscar Larm, Warren; 6-F. P. Mullens, Madison; 7-V. D. Sexton, Greene, and J. W. Raub, Monroe; 8-L. M. Vogler, Bartholomew; 9-John J. Brown, Spencer; and 10-John G. Klein, Jennings.

1920

1-J. A. Warren; 2-R. L. Thompson, LaGrange County; 3-E. E. Reynolds; 4-W. H. Settle, Wells; 5-Oscar Larm; 6-Earl Crawford, Wayne County; 7-J. W. Raub; 8-L. M. Vogler; 9-John J. Brown; 10-Charles S. Douglas, Ohio.

1921

1-J. A. Warren; 2-R. L. Thompson; 3-E. E. Reynolds (replaced in May by C. S. Moore, Clinton County); 4-W. H. Settle; 5-Oscar Larm; 6-Earl Crawford; 7-J. W. Raub; 8-L. M. Vogler; 9-J. W. Gwaltney, Posey; 10-Charles S. Douglas.

1922

1-I. H. Hull, LaPorte County; 2-R. L. Thompson; 3-Burton D. Honan, Carroll; 4-W. H. Settle;

5-Oscar Larm; 6-Earl Crawford; 7-Addison
Drake, Sullivan; 8-L. M. Vogler; 9-J. W.
Gwaltney; 10-Charles S. Douglas.

1923

1-I. H. Hull; 2-W. H. Robbins, Whitley County;
3-Burton D. Honan; 4-W. H. Settle; 5-Oscar
Larm; 6-L. A. Pittenger, Delaware; 7-Addison
Drake; 8-James K. Mason, Fayette; 9-J. W.
Gwaltney; 10-W. Clyde Martin, Harrison. (In
April, L. L. Needler of Grant County was
named fourth district director to fill the vacancy
left by the new president, W. H. Settle. In May,
George W. Trautman, Ripley County, was
elected tenth district director.)

1924

1-I. H. Hull; 2-W. H. Robbins; 3-Burton D.
Honan; 4-L. L. Needler; 5-Oscar Larm; 6-L. A.
Pittenger; 7-Addison Drake; 8-James K. Mason;
9-J. W. Gwaltney; 10-George W. Trautman.

1925

1-I. H. Hull; 2-W. H. Robbins; 3-Burton D.
Honan; 4-L. L. Needler; 5-Oscar Larm;
6-Everett Hunt, Wayne County; 7-Addison
Drake; 8-James K. Mason; 9-J. W. Gwaltney;
10-Everett McClure, Dearborn.

1926

1-Paul Engle, Pulaski County; 2-W. H. Robbins; 3-Guy McMullen, White; 4-James B. Cummins, Jay; 5-Oscar Larm; 6-Everett Hunt; 7-Addison Drake; 8-James K. Mason; 9-J. W. Gwaltney; 10-Everett McClure.

1927

1-Paul Engle; 2-W. H. Robbins; 3-Guy McMullen; 4-James B. Cummins; 5-Oscar Larm; 6-Everett Hunt; 7-Addison Drake; 8-James K. Mason; 9-J. W. Gwaltney; 10-Everett McClure.

1928

1-C. R. Benjamin, Lake County, replaced Engle in December; 2-W. H. Robbins; 3-Guy McMullen; 4-James B. Cummins; 5-Oscar Larm; 6-Everett Hunt; 7-Addison Drake; 8-James K. Mason; 9-J. W. Gwaltney; 10-Howard Atcheson, Scott.

1929

1-C. R. Benjamin; 2-W. H. Robbins; 3-Guy McMullen; 4-James B. Cummins; 5-Oscar Larm; 6-Everett Hunt; 7-Addison Drake; 8-James K. Mason; 9-J. W. Gwaltney; 10-Howard Atcheson.

1930

1-C. R. Benjamin; 2-W. H. Robbins; 3-Guy Mc-Mullen; 4-James B. Cummins; 5-Oscar Larm; 6-Everett Hunt; 7-Addison Drake; 8-James K. Mason; 9-J. W. Gwaltney; 10-Howard Atcheson.

1931

1-C. R. Benjamin; 2-W. H. Robbins; 3-Arthur E. Arnott, Jasper County, replaced Mullen in December; 4-James B. Cummins; 5-Oscar Larm; 6-Everett Hunt; 7-Addison Drake; 8-James K. Mason; 9-J. W. Gwaltney; 10-Howard Atcheson.

1932

1-C. R. Benjamin; 2-W. H. Robbins; 3-Arthur E. Arnott; 4-James B. Cummins; 5-Oscar Larm; 6-Everett Hunt; 7-Addison Drake; 8-James K. Mason; 9-J. W. Gwaltney; 10-Howard Atcheson.

1933

1-C. R. Benjamin; 2-W. H. Robbins; 3-Arthur E. Arnott; 4-James B. Cummins; 5-Oscar Larm; 6-Everett Hunt; 7-Addison Drake; 8-James K. Mason; 9-Floyd J. Hemmer, Dubois County,

replaced Gwaltney in April; 10-Howard
Atcheson.

1934

1-C. R. Benjamin; 2-W. H. Robbins; 3-Arthur
E. Arnott; 4-James B. Cummins; 5-Oscar Larm;
6-Everett Hunt; 7-Addison Drake; 8-James K.
Mason; 9-Floyd J. Hemmer; 10-Howard
Atcheson.

1935

1-C. R. Benjamin; 2-W. H. Robbins; 3-Arthur
E. Arnott; 4-James B. Cummins; 5-Oscar Larm;
6-Everett Hunt; 7-Addison Drake; 8-Maurice
Douglas, Shelby County; 9-Henry Whittinghill,
Warrick, replaced Hemmer who had became a
state senator; 10-Howard Atcheson.

1936

1-C. R. Benjamin; 2-W. H. Robbins, who was
replaced in November by Larry Brandon,
DeKalb County; 3-Arthur E. Arnott; 4-James
B. Cummins; 5-Oscar Larm; 6-Everett Hunt;
7-Addison Drake; 8-Maurice Douglas; 9-Henry
Whittinghill; 10-Howard Atcheson.

1937

1-C. R. Benjamin, who was replaced in June
by Adolph Tack, Pulaski County; 2-Albert

Yoder, DeKalb; 3-Arthur E. Arnott; 4-James B. Cummins; 5-Oscar Larm; 6-Everett Hunt; 7-Addison Drake; 8-Maurice Douglas; 9-Henry Whittinghill; 10-George Elliott, Ohio.

1938

1-Adolph Tack; 2-Albert Yoder; 3-Arthur E. Arnott; 4-James B. Cummins; 5-J. Walter Thompson, Montgomery County; 6-Everett Hunt; 7-Addison Drake; 8-Maurice Douglas; 9-Floyd Moye, Posey County; 10-George Elliott.

1939

1-Oliver Cannon, Starke County; 2-Albert Yoder; 3-Arthur E. Arnott; 4-James B. Cummins; 5-J. Walter Thompson; 6-Everett Hunt was replaced in December by H. D. Gordon, Henry County; 7-Addison Drake; 8-Maurice Douglas; 9-Floyd Moye; 10-George Elliott.

1940

1-Oliver Cannon; 2-Albert Yoder; 3-Arthur E. Arnott; 4-James B. Cummins; 5-J. Walter Thompson; 6-H. D. Gordon was replaced in December by Harry Modlin, Henry County; 7-Addison Drake; 8-Maurice Douglas; 9-Floyd Moye; 10-George Elliott.

1941

1-Oliver Cannon; 2-Albert Yoder; 3-Arthur E. Arnott; 4-James B. Cummins; 5-J. Walter Thompson; 6-Harry Modlin; 7-Addison Drake; 8-Maurice Douglas; 9-Floyd Moye; 10-George Elliott.

1942

1-Oliver Cannon; 2-Albert Yoder; 3-Arthur E. Arnott; 4-James B. Cummins was replaced by C. E. Moseley, Miami County, in November; 5-J. Walter Thompson; 6-Harry Modlin; 7-Addison Drake; 8-Maurice Douglas; 9-Floyd Moye; 10-George Elliott.

1943

1-Oliver Cannon; 2-Albert Yoder; 3-Arthur E. Arnott; 4-C. E. Moseley; 5-J. Walter Thompson; 6-Harry Modlin; 7-Addison Drake; 8-Maurice Douglas; 9-Floyd Moye; 10-George Elliott.

1944

1-Oliver Cannon; 2-Albert Yoder; 3-Arthur E. Arnott; 4-C. E. Moseley; 5-J. Walter Thompson; 6-Frank Scott, Wayne County, was elected in November to replace Modlin; 7-Addison Drake; 8-Maurice Douglas; 9-Floyd Moye; 10-George Elliott.

1945

1-Oliver Cannon was replaced in December by V. H. Schalliol, St. Joseph County; 2-Albert Yoder; 3-Arthur E. Arnott; 4-C. E. Moseley; 5-J. Walter Thompson; 6-Frank Scott; 7-Addison Drake; 8-George Doup, Bartholomew County, was elected in October to succeed Douglas; 9-Lowell Taylor, Gibson County, was elected in March to succeed Moye; 10-George Elliott.

1946

1-V. H. Schalliol; 2-Elmer Kolmerten, Allen County, was elected in December to succeed Albert Yoder; 3-Arthur E. Arnott; 4-C. E. Moseley; 5-J. Walter Thompson; 6-Frank Scott; 7-Addison Drake; 8-George Doup; 9-Lowell Taylor; 10-George Elliott.

1947

1-V. H. Schalliol was succeeded in December by Emil Bannwart, LaPorte County; 2-Elmer Kolmerten; 3-Arthur E. Arnott; 4-C. E. Moseley; 5-J. Walter Thompson; 6-Frank Scott; 7-Addison Drake; 8-George Doup; 9-Lowell Taylor; 10-George Elliott.

1948

1-Emil Bannwart; 2-Elmer Kolmerten;

3-Arthur E. Arnott; 4-C. E. Moseley; 5-J. Walter
Thompson; 6-Ernest Freeman, Delaware
County; 7-Addison Drake; 8-George Doup;
9-Lowell Taylor; 10-George Elliott.

1949

1-Emil Bannwart; 2-Elmer Kolmerten;
3-Arthur E. Arnott; 4-C. E. Moseley; 5-J. Walter
Thompson; 6-Ernest Freeman; 7-after the death
of Mr. Drake, Clarence McCormick, Knox
County, was elected in November; 8-George
Doup; 9-Lowell Taylor; 10-George Elliott.

1950

1-Emil Bannwart; 2-Elmer Kolmerten;
3-Arthur E. Arnott; 4-C. E. Moseley; 5-J. Walter
Thompson; 6-Ernest Freeman; 7-Wayne Mann,
Orange County, was elected after McCormick
was appointed Under Secretary of Agriculture
in August; 8-George Doup; 9-Lowell Taylor;
10-George Elliott.

1951

1-Emil Bannwart; 2-Elmer Kolmerten;
3-Arthur E. Arnott; 4-C. E. Moseley; 5-J. Walter
Thompson; 6-Ernest Freeman; 7-Wayne Mann;
8-Glen Retherford, Rush County, was elected
when Doup was named head of the livestock

department, IFB, in March; 9-Lowell Taylor;
10-George Elliott.

1952

1-Emil Bannwart; 2-Elmer Kolmerten;
3-Arthur E. Arnott; 4-C. E. Moseley; 5-J. Walter
Thompson; 6-Ernest Freeman; 7-Wayne Mann;
8-Glen Retherford; 9-Lowell Taylor; 10-George
Elliott.

1953

1-Emil Bannwart; 2-Elmèr Kolmerten;
3-Arthur E. Arnott; 4-Carl Bowman, Blackford
County, succeeded C. E. Moseley in November;
5-J. Walter Thompson; 6-Ernest Freeman;
7-Wayne Mann; 8-Glen Retherford; 9-Lowell
Taylor; 10-George Elliott.

1954

1-Emil Bannwart; 2-Elmer Kolmerten was
succeeded in November by George Neff,
Elkhart County; 3-Arthur E. Arnott; 4-Carl
Bowman; 5-J. Walter Thompson; 6-Ernest
Freeman; 7-Wayne Mann; 8-Glen Retherford;
9-Lowell Taylor; 10-George Elliott.

1955

1-Emil Bannwart; 2-George Neff, 3-Arthur E.

Arnott; 4-Carl Bowman; 5-J. Walter Thompson; 6-Ernest Freeman; 7-Wayne Mann; 8-Glen Retherford; 9-Lowell Taylor; 10-George Elliott.

1956

1-Emil Bannwart; 2-George Neff; 3-Arthur E. Arnott; 4-Carl Bowman; 5-J. Walter Thompson; 6-Ernest Freeman; 7-Wayne Mann; 8-Glen Retherford; 9-Lowell Taylor; 10-George Elliott.

1957

1-Emil Bannwart; 2-George Neff; 3-Arthur E. Arnott; 4-Carl Bowman; 5-J. Walter Thompson; 6-Ernest Freeman; 7-in November, Edward Kuhn, Knox County, succeeded Mann; 8-George Ruschhaupt, Shelby County, was elected upon the death of Mr. Retherford; 9-Lowell Taylor; 10-Linville Bryant, Ripley County, was elected in November.

1958

1-Emil Bannwart was succeeded in November by Charles Riddle, Marshall County; 2-George Neff; 3-in November, Lawrence Holloway, Clinton County, succeeded Arnott; 4-Carl Bowman; 5-Harmon Rogers, Montgomery County, succeeded Thompson in November; 6-Ernest Freeman; 7-Edward Kuhn; 8-George

Ruschhaupt; 9-Lowell Taylor; 10-Linville Bryant.

1959

1-Charles Riddle; 2-George Neff; 3-Lawrence Holloway; 4-Carl Bowman; 5-Harmon Rogers; 6-Ernest Freeman, who died in October to be succeeded by Evan Wilson; 7-Edward Kuhn; 8-George Ruschhaupt; 9-Lowell Taylor; 10-Linville Bryant.

1960-1961

1-Charles Riddle; 2-George Neff; 3-Lawrence Holloway; 4-Carl Bowman; 5-Harmon Rogers; 6-Evan Wilson; 7-Edward Kuhn; 8-George Ruschhaupt; 9-Lowell Taylor; 10-Linville Bryant.

1962

1-Charles Riddle; 2-George Neff; 3-Lawrence Holloway; 4-Carlin Schoeff, Blackford County, was elected in November to succeed Bowman; 5-Harmon Rogers; 6-Evan Wilson; 7-Edward Kuhn; 8-George Ruschhaupt; 9-Lowell Taylor; 10-Linville Bryant.

1963

1-Charles Riddle; 2-George Neff; 3-Lawrence Holloway; 4-Carlin Schoeff; 5-Harmon Rogers;

6-Evan Wilson; 7-Edward Kuhn; 8-George Ruschhaupt; 9-Warren Wheaton, Pike County, was elected to fill vacancy created by Lowell Taylor's death in January; 10-Linville Bryant.

1964

1-Charles Riddle; 2-George Neff; 3-Lawrence Holloway; 4-Carlin Schoeff; 5-Harmon Rogers; 6-Evan Wilson; 7-Edward Kuhn; 8-George Ruschhaupt; 9-Warren Wheaton; 10-Linville Bryant.

1965

1-Oris Bedenkop, LaPorte County; 2-George Neff; 3-Lawrence Holloway; 4-Carlin Schoeff; 5-Marion Cowan, Montgomery County; 6-Evan Wilson; 7-Edward Kuhn; 8-George Ruschhaupt; 9-Warren Wheaton; 10-Linville Bryant.

1966-

1-Oris Bedenkop; 2-George Neff; 3-Lawrence Holloway; 4-Carlin Schoeff; 5-Marion Cowan; 6-Virgil Cline, Delaware County; 7-Edward Kuhn; 8-George Ruschhaupt; 9-Warren Wheaton; 10-Linville Bryant.

COUNTY FARM BUREAU MEMBERSHIP, NOVEMBER 13, 1967

Adams	1,232	Lawrence	2,168
Allen	4,173	Madison	3,771
Bartholomew	2,765	Marion	5,936
Benton	1,177	Marshall	1,853
Blackford	1,017	Martin	781
Boone	1,759	Miami	1,397
Brown	513	Monroe	1,682
Carroll	1,706	Montgomery	2,092
Cass	1,764	Morgan	1,699
Clark	1,470	Newton	844
Clay	1,433	Noble	1,614
Clinton	1,804	Ohio	263
Crawford	426	Orange	1,030
Daviess	1,327	Owen	564
Dearborn	1,450	Parke	1,210
Decatur	1,366	Perry	509
DeKalb	1,541	Pike	652
Delaware	4,158	Porter	2,326
Dubois	1,213	Posey	1,883
Elkhart	3,157	Pulaski	964
Fayette	1,019	Putnam	1,030
Floyd	813	Randolph	1,082
Fountain	1,046	Ripley	1,398
Franklin	999	Rush	1,331
Fulton	967	Scott	748
Gibson	1,086	Shelby	1,688
Grant	2,664	St. Joseph	3,019
Greene	1,409	Spencer	1,131
Hamilton	2,007	Starke	1,075
Hancock	1,812	Steuben	1,570
Harrison	1,853	Sullivan	1,266
Hendricks	1,466	Switzerland	377
Henry	1,914	Tippecanoe	3,202
Howard	2,631	Tipton	1,843
Huntington	1,955	Union	418
Jackson	1,700	Vanderburgh	2,635
Jasper	1,395	Vermillion	707
Jay	941	Vigo	2,497
Jefferson	1,214	Wabash	2,837
Jennings	1,031	Warren	956
Johnson	2,336	Warrick	791
Knox	1,511	Washington	1,170
Kosciusko	1,846	Wayne	2,669
LaGrange	1,099	Wells	2,003
Lake	4,384	White	1,196
LaPorte	3,101	Whitley	1,635

State Total 153,168

INDEX